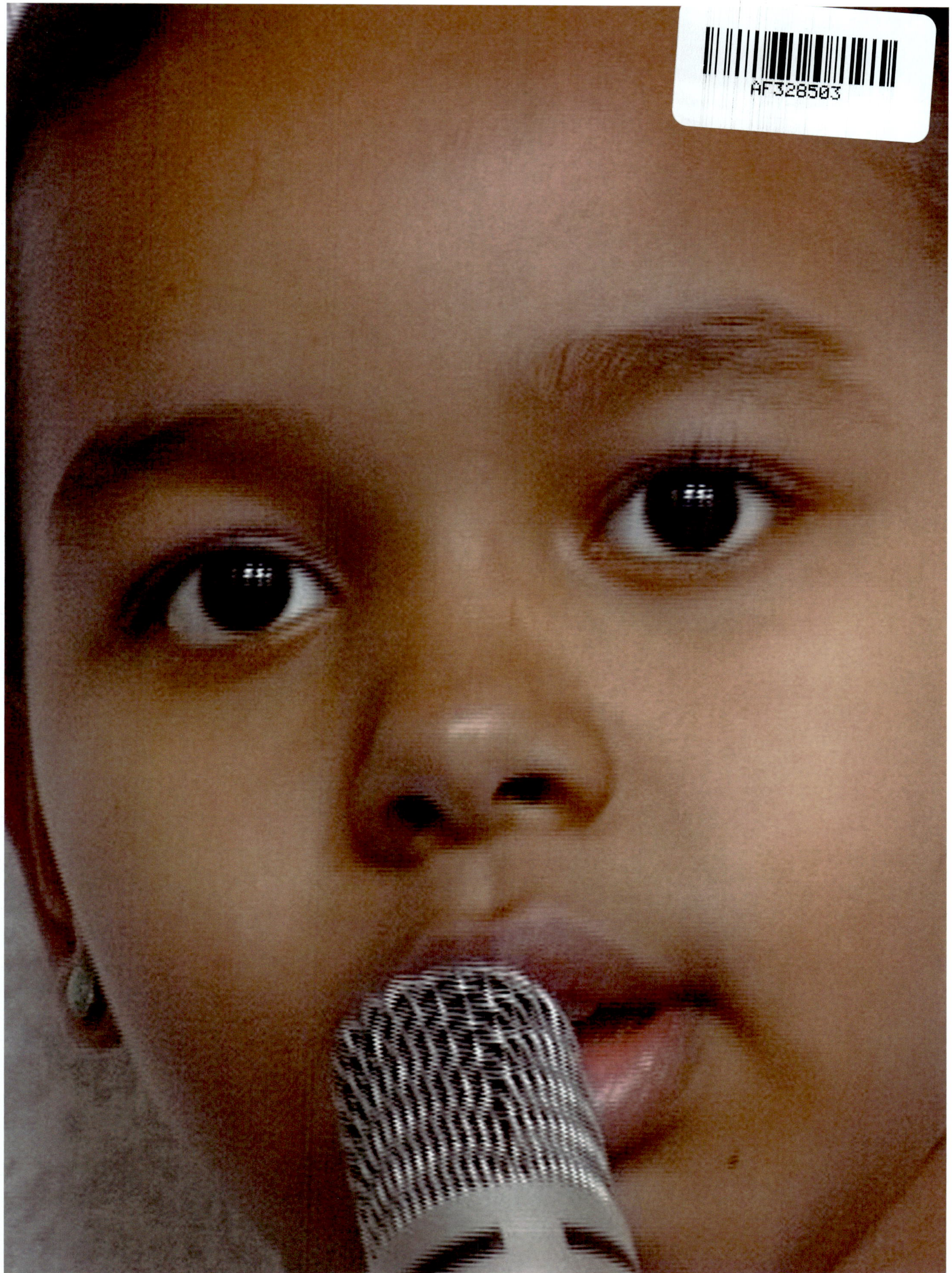

Read page 80

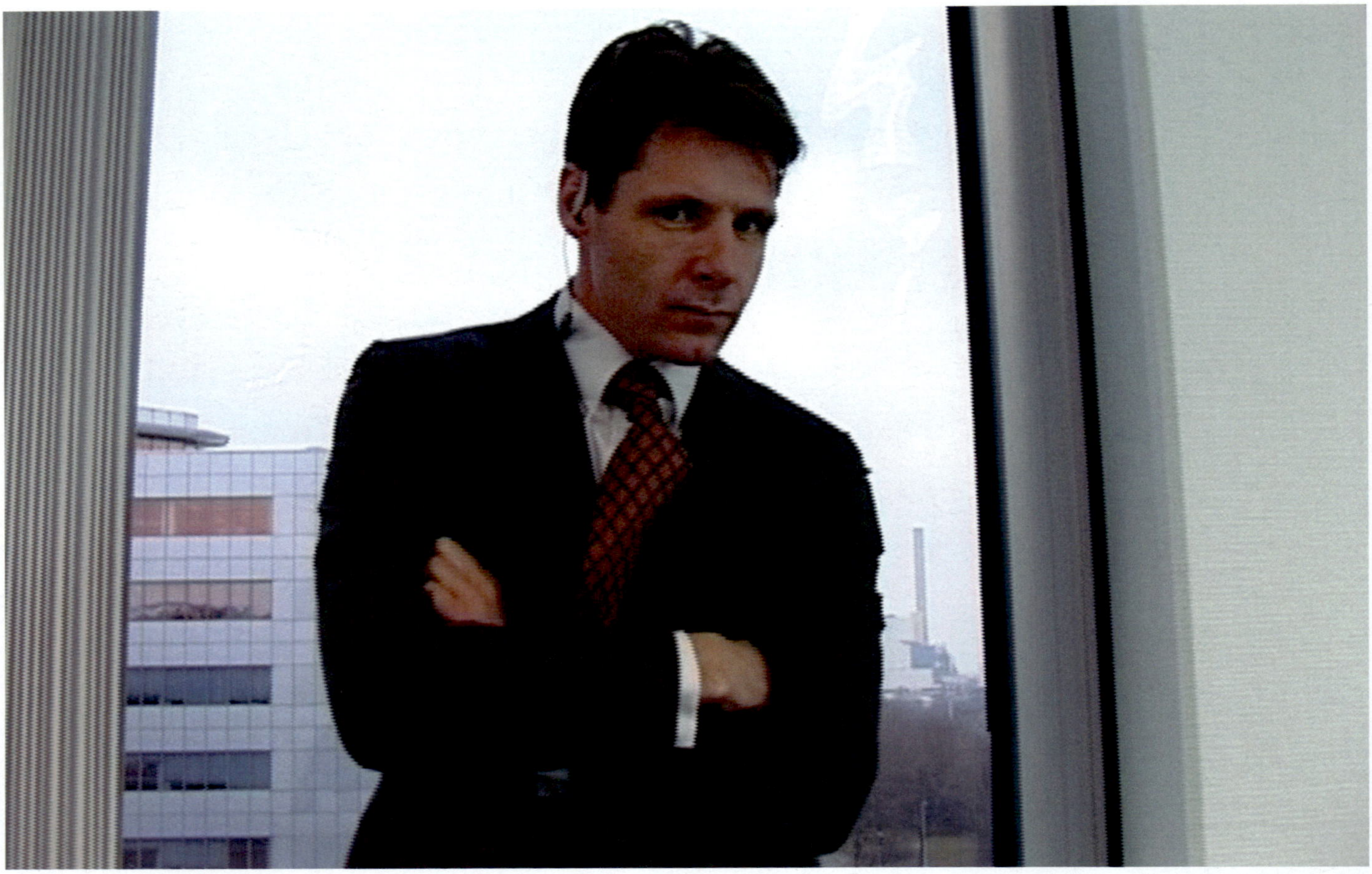

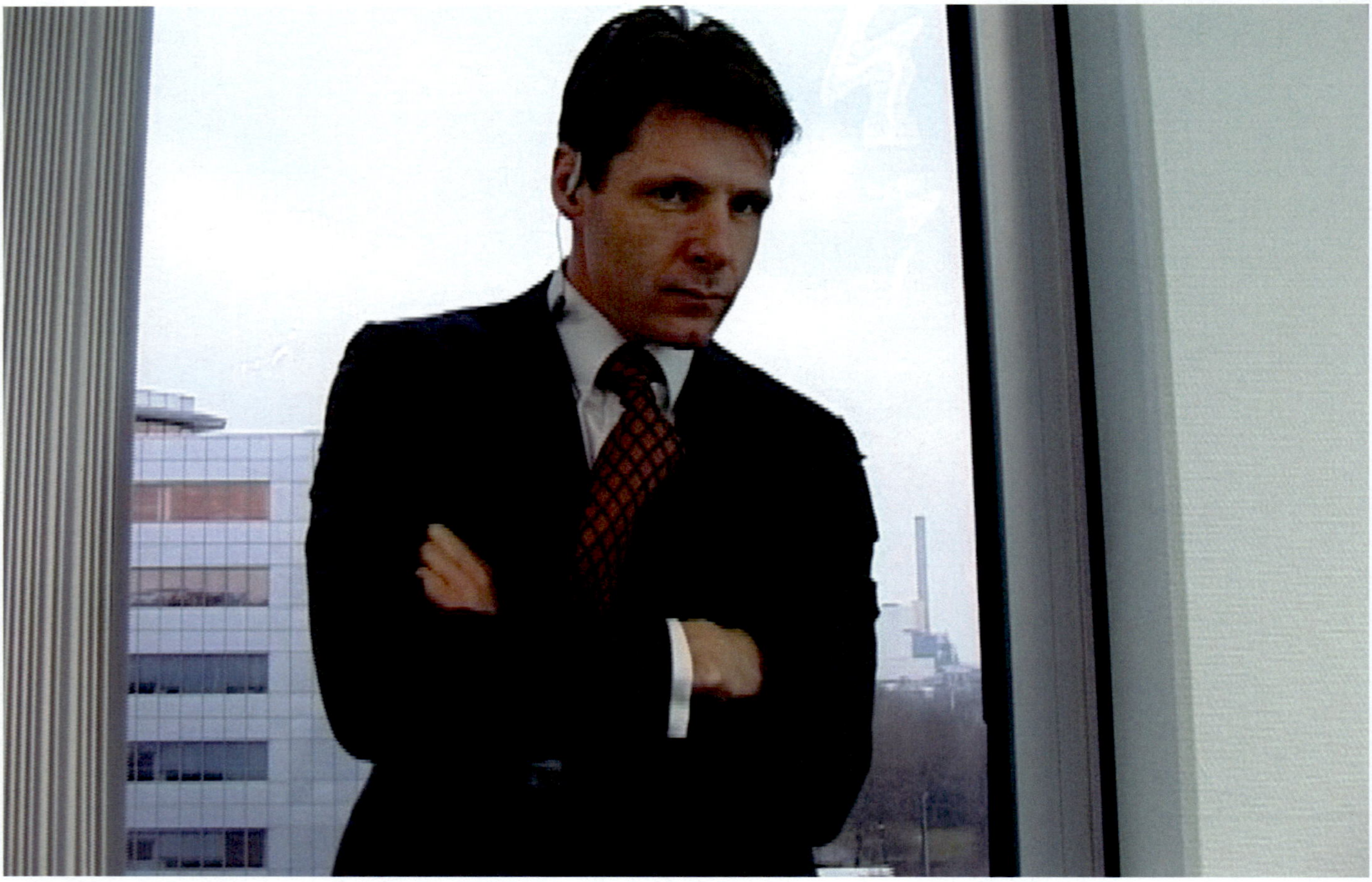

Read page 91

JULIKA RUDELIUS

LOOKING AT THE OTHER

FIVE VIDEO WORKS

VALIZ, AMSTERDAM

CONTENTS

ESSAY

CINEMA'S DOPPELGÄNGER

REMARKS ON TWO WORKS BY JULIKA RUDELIUS

SVEN LÜTTICKEN

CINEMA'S DOPPELGÄNGER
Remarks on Two Works by Julika Rudelius

Tagged (2003) and *Economic Primacy* (2005) are two
closely related works by Julika Rudelius. *Economic
Primacy* is a double projection in which Dutch
businessmen expound their convictions and preju-
dices, whereas *Tagged* focuses on young men, mainly
of Moroccan descent, and all living in Amsterdam.
Tagged consists not of two but of three aligned and
immediately adjacent projections, but the general
structure of the works is the same. Both show members
of a group who share certain values and a *habitus*,
and in both cases the members of this group are shown
in an abstract, generic space: a bare hotel room in
Tagged, and a bland office in *Economic Primacy*. In
both works, a shot usually shows only one person in
this interior (in *Tagged* there are brief shots of two
boys together). Double or triple projection enables
Rudelius to practise a kind of synchronic montage
that establishes connections between the various protagonists, between two or more images — in addition
to the diachronic montage between two shots within
one and the same projection. While the coexistence of

these two forms of montage is by now rather common, as multiple projection is ubiquitous in contemporary video art, the way in which Rudelius deploys double and triple projection is specific to her practice.

Long before double projection became a staple of film and video art, Heinrich Wölfflin had established the double projection of slides as an indispensable tool for art-history lectures. Juxtaposing slides of different works of art — and the related method of juxtaposing illustrations in books and journals — offered Wölfflin and others a chance to define and distinguish between styles such as the 'classical' and the 'baroque', or the linear and the painterly; it also facilitated the comparative analysis of specific works and the reconstruction of artists' oeuvres. In this way, double projection helped to increase art historians' skill at appraising works of art, thus providing crucial services to the art market. In the 1960s and 1970s, both single and multiple slide projection were also adopted by artists such as Marcel Broodthaers, who turned the methods of art history against itself, creating sequences and juxtapositions of images that sabotaged traditional stylistic or iconographic attempts to come to terms with them.[1] But the projection of two parallel streams of moving images in double film or video projection gives the viewers much less control over the material than even the most absurd — and the fastest — slide projections. This was exploited by the expanded cinema movement in the late 1960s and early 1970s, when filmmakers and artists sought to introduce more stimulating and activating participatory modes of spectatorship than that of passive consumption in the standard cinema *dispositif*. In this context, double projection became a kind of minimal form of expanded cinema.[2]

1 On the slide projector in art and art history, see Pamela M. Lee, 'Split Decision', in: *Artforum* vol. XLIII, no. 3 (November 2004), pp. 47-48.

2 A recent overview and analysis of expanded cinema is provided by *X-Screen: Filmische Installationen und Aktionen der Sechziger- und Siebzigerjahre*, exhib. cat. Museum Moderner Kunst Stiftung Ludwig Wien, 2004.

3 In an early text on Warhol's films, Gregory Battcock denied that Warhol was at all preoccupied with 'questions of comparison and time in the cinema image' with his double projections. Gregory Battcock, 'Four Films by Andy Warhol', in: *The New American Cinema* (ed. Gregory Battcock), New York, Dutton, 1967, p. 249.

Andy Warhol, who was among the artists and film-makers who pioneered multiple film projection in the late 1960s, emphasized the aleatory, Cagean potential of double projection — its capability to create unforeseen combinations that need not make sense in the way of classical montage. As with the Exploding Plastic Inevitable, Warhol aimed at sensory confusion and a kind of blank exhilaration rather than analytical comparisons.[3] By contrast, Harun Farocki's recent double video projections represent a starkly different position: like Jean-Luc Godard, and along the same lines as Sergei Eisenstein and other Russian montage theorists and practitioners, Farocki conceives of montage as a critical tool, as a dialectical procedure in which images function as thesis and antithesis. Although Julika Rudelius seems to curtail the possibilities for synchronic multiple-projection montage in an extreme and arbitrary way by juxtaposing images with identical settings and highly similar people, her work still uses double projection as an analytical device, and in Farocki's case this is an analysis-in-movement that can never congeal into two static pictures that can be con-templated and dissected at will; any constellation of images and sounds in these works is ephemeral.

In his video essay *Schnittstelle* (1995), Farocki puts double video projection not so much in the lineage of expanded cinema pieces by Warhol, Dan Graham or Valie Export, but rather presents it as a consequence of video editing, which replaced the laborious splic-ing of film strips with the possibility of seeing and selecting simultaneously from two or more video images. While these images will usually be edited into a single-channel video, the video-editing

4 Tim Griffin, 'Viewfinder', in: *Artforum* vol. XLIII, no. 3 (November 2004), p. 163.

booth itself witnesses a constant parallel montage of multiple images. Perhaps this, rather than the linear product that comes out of it, is the true form of video montage, in which – as Farocki puts it in *Schnittstelle* – an image is not commented on with words but with another image. In a way arguing like an avant-garde version of Wölfflin – if such a thing is imaginable – Farocki elsewhere states that 'today there's always the image, and then the image being read in terms of what's next to it'.[4] Using the characteristics of video editing as the basis for his double-channel video installations, especially *Ich glaubte Gefangene zu sehen* (2000) and the recent *Eye/Machine* trilogy, Farocki creates a dialectical tension between new and archival footage – such as images from contemporary high-tech prisons and footage from old slapstick films – as well as spoken and written language. This tension is never resolved in simple statements or linear argument; his work is more open-ended than Russian revolutionary film, not leading to a synthesis that represents the Party line.

What is remarkable about Rudelius' multi-channel works is the apparent refusal to fully use the possibilities double or triple projection offers, its opportunities for dialectical combinations of apparently incommensurate images: if one can use images to comment on other images, then why are her images so utterly alike? Both in *Tagged* and in *Economic Primacy*, Rudelius' footage has been shot in a single location: a hotel room and an office, respectively. Both spaces are bland and generic, with white walls and minimal furniture. Both in *Tagged* and *Economic Primacy*, the people in these spaces are also rather alike. The youths in *Tagged* all spend a lot of money on clothes from certain brands, which they show in the video, while the businessmen all wear roughly similar suits and talk similar business talk about taking risks and being different from the passive masses. Even Warhol's *The Chelsea Girls* is varied by comparison — the apparently monotonous conceit of women talking in various rooms of the Chelsea Hotel being relieved by changes from colour to black and white, by the differences between the flamboyant protagonist and various other factors. A work that resembles Rudelius' two works more closely is Rineke Dijkstra's *The Buzz Club, Liverpool, UK/Mysteryworld, Zaandam, NL* (1996-1997), a two-channel video projection consisting of footage — shot in two clubs — of teenagers dancing, kissing or dreaming in front of a white background. While the piece invites one to compare the various dress codes and individual attitudes, it also creates a montage of swelling and receding rhythms — both on the soundtrack and visually — that emphasizes the musical and, in a sense, formalist aspect of double projection.

Tagged and *Economic Primacy* seem to foster a more detached form of spectatorship than Dijkstra's *Buzz Club/Mysteryworld*: all the attention is focused on dress codes, behavioural patterns and modes of speech, and there is no music or dancing — however industrialized and monotonous the music and the dancing may be — to offer relief from their uniformity. The protagonists in both Rudelius' videos seem to be stuck in a world of sameness and repetition, in a world of boys and men cast from similar moulds. In this sense, *Tagged* and *Economic Primacy* are somewhat less explicit variations on Rudelius' three-channel video *Plush* (2001). Shown on monitors rather than projected, *Plush* is an exercise in understated horror: the video depicts three uncannily similar blonde girls, or young women, who seem to be stuck in a

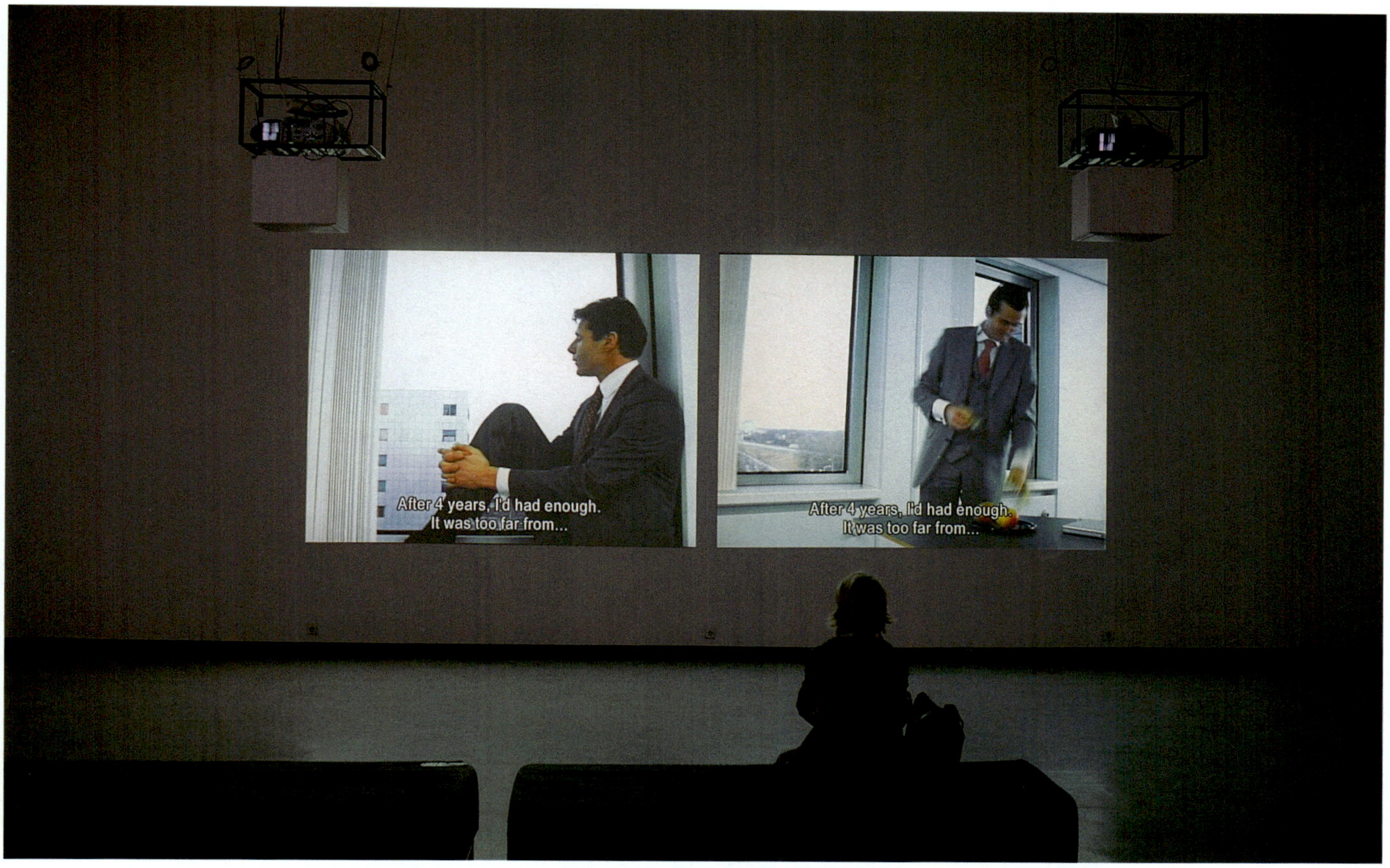

Economic Primacy, Contemporary Art Centre (CAC), Vilnius, Lithuania, 2005

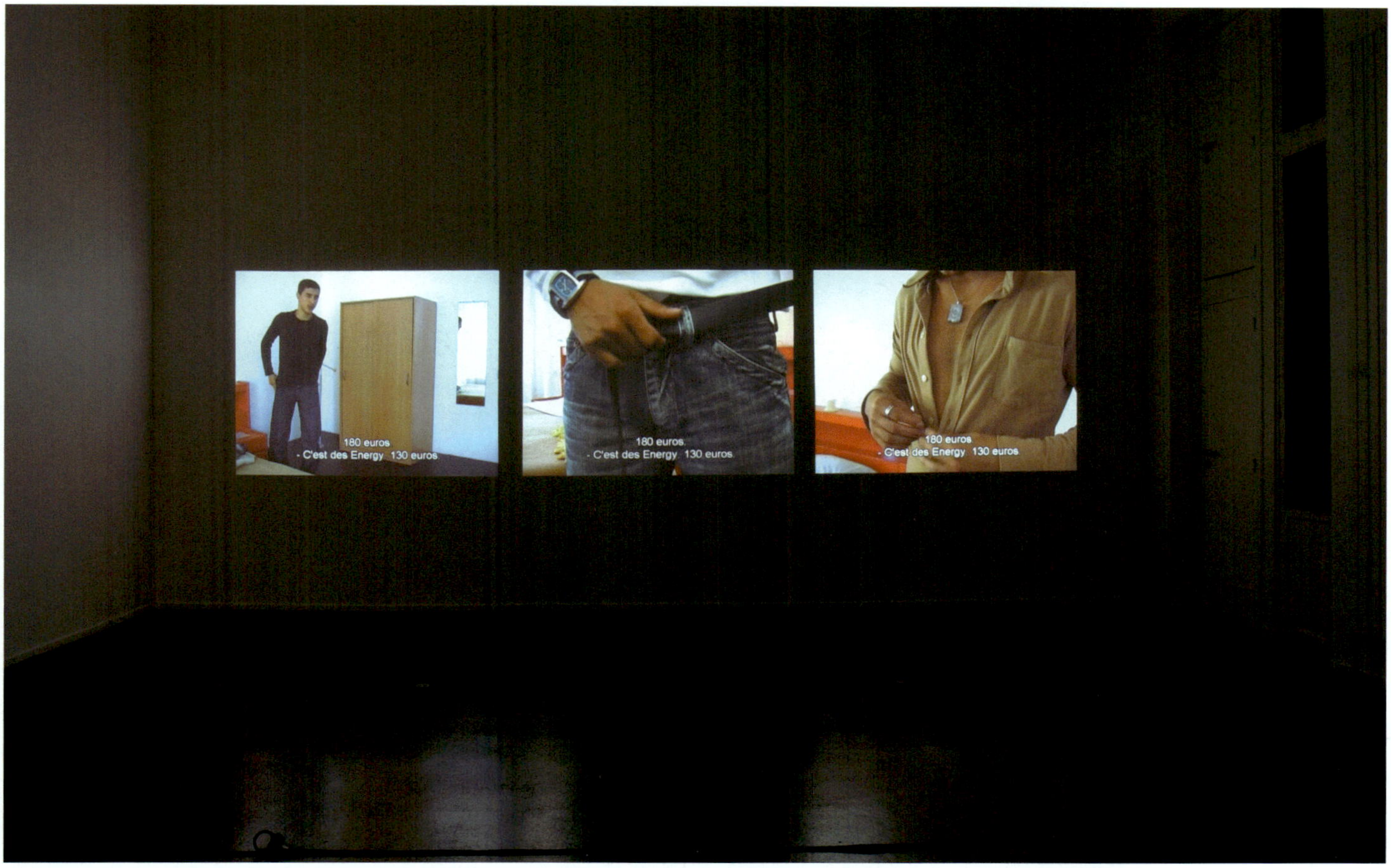

Tagged, Centre Culturel Suisse, Paris, France, 2004

When I change my clothes, when I do my hair, when I see a mirror...

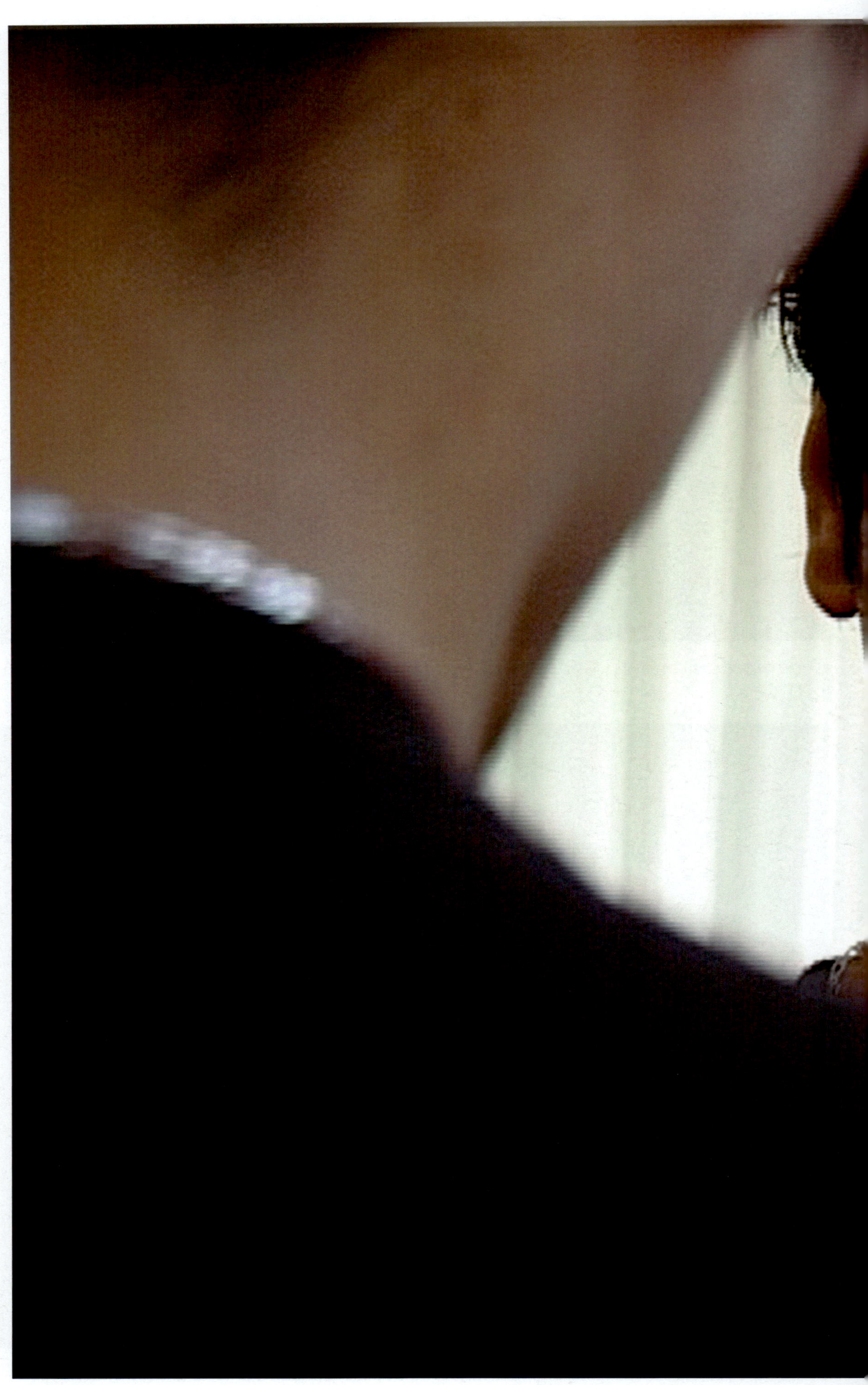

Read page 56

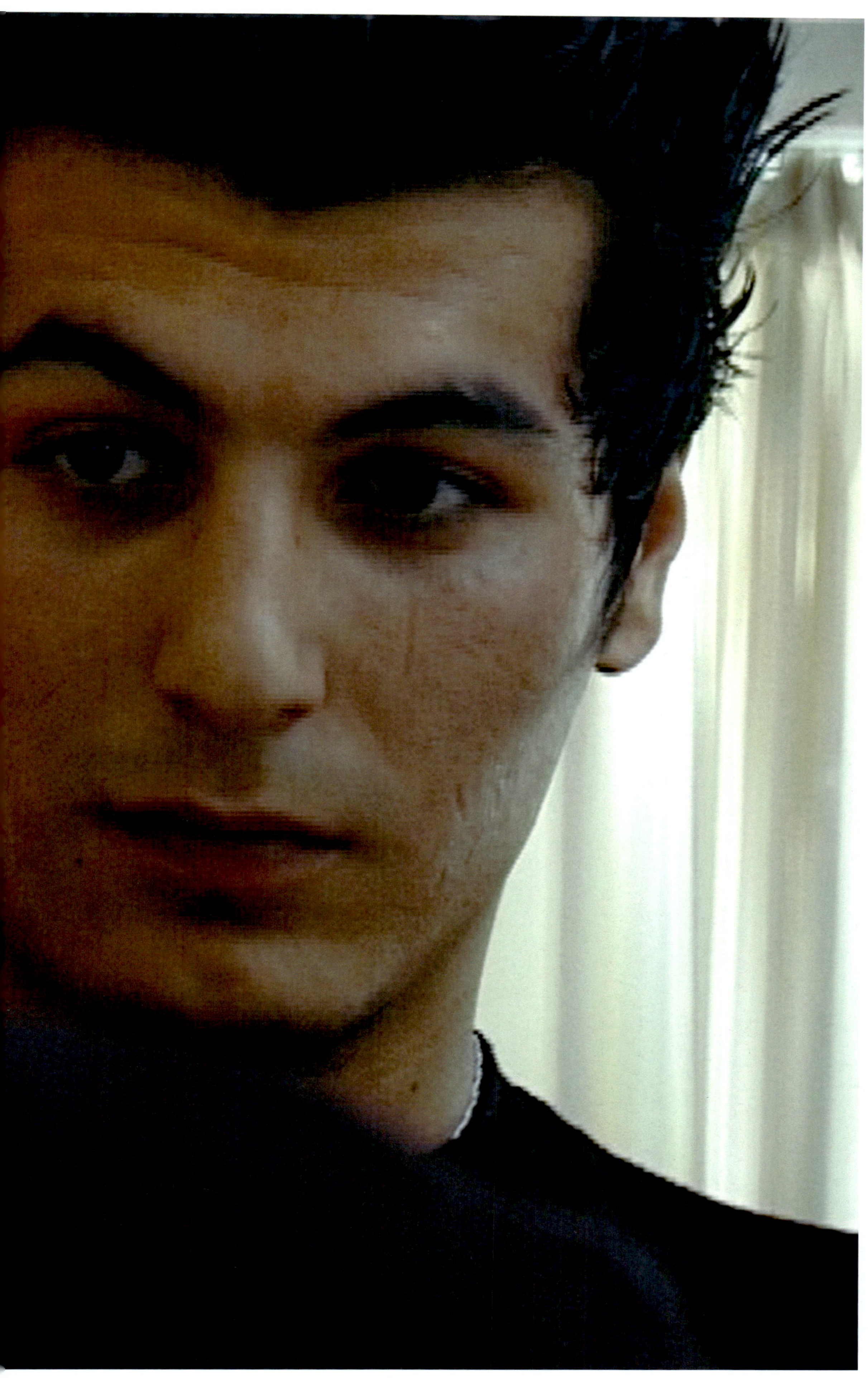

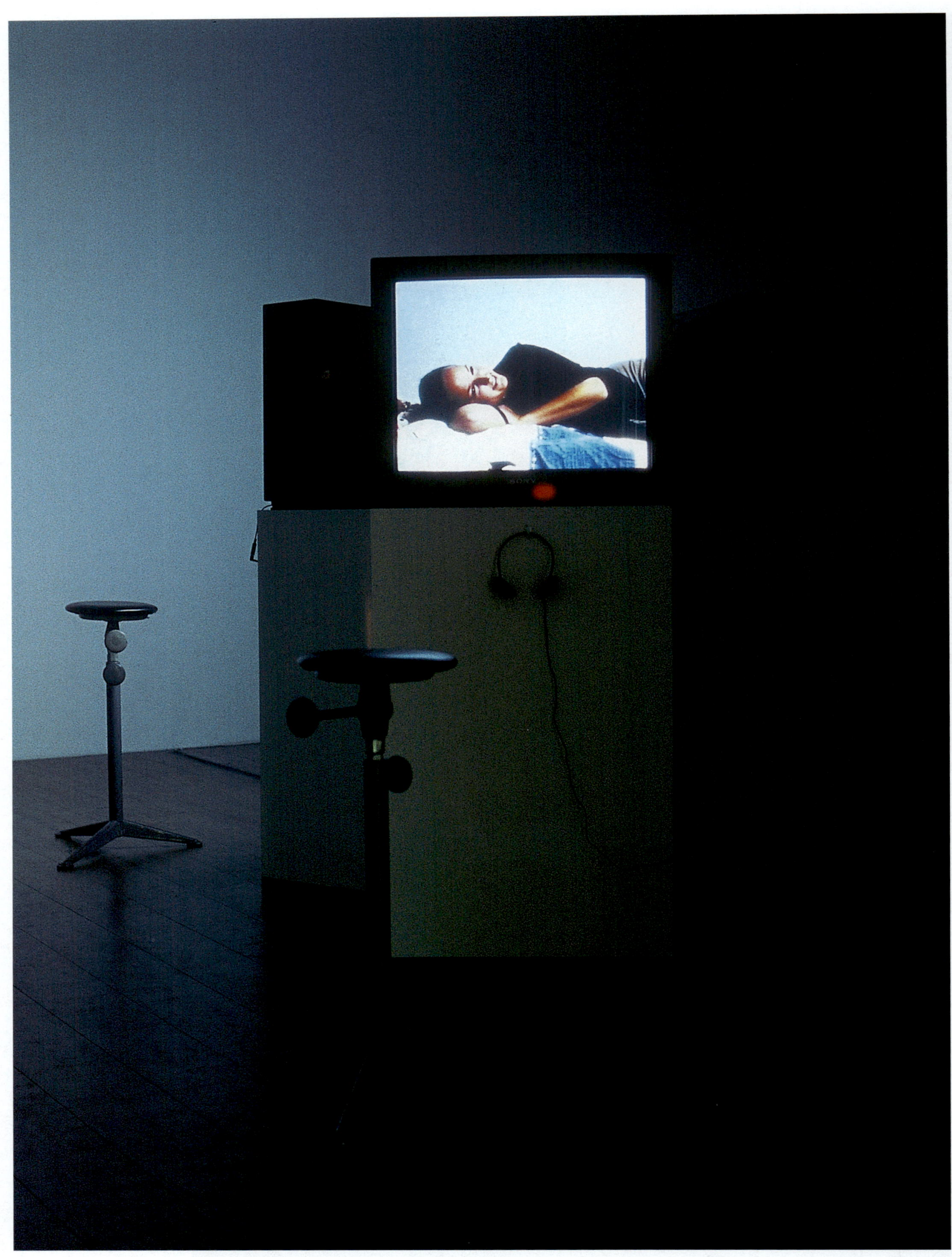

Plush, Stedelijk Museum Bureau Amsterdam, Netherlands, 2001

sugar-coated girlish universe symbolized by plush animals on their beds. The counterpart of *Plush* is *Train*, in which a group of teenage boys discusses girls and sex during a train ride. Their behaviour is as stereotypical and conformist as the girls' very different behaviour, but *Plush* differs from *Train* in that its effect is uncanny. The boys are part of the same group and thus show comparable behaviour, but the girls, each shown in a stereotypical girl's room, are triple doppelgängers – they are in fact actual triplets, though the viewer is left to guess whether this is the case, or whether the similarity is the result of very precise casting.

The doppelgänger motif, prominent in western literature since the late eighteenth century, is symptomatic of the fear that modern man – historically, most doppelgängers seem to be male, as the male subject was the subject par excellence – is under attack, under threat of disintegration. As society becomes more and more regulated and complex, man becomes a cog in a machine rather than an individual, a man of the crowd dressed the same as the others, essentially becoming part of a collective of doubles. Increasingly, the human body was also supplemented and even replaced by machines acting as the body's functional, mechanical doubles, while the new medium of cinema created moving doppelgängers of people's appearance – turning them into shadows of their own celluloid representations.[5] 'The feeling of strangeness that overcomes the actor before the camera, as Pirandello describes it, is basically of the same kind as the estrangement felt before one's own image in the mirror. But now the reflected image has become separable, transportable.'[6] It is not surprising that cinema eagerly

5 See Peter Weibel, 'Phantom Painting', in: *New Paintings for the Mirror Room and Archive in a Studio off the Courtyard by David Reed*, exhib. cat. Neue Galerie Graz am Landesmuseum Joanneum, 1996, pp. 49-55.

6 Walter Benjamin, 'Das Kunstwerk im Zeitalter seiner technischen Reproduzierbarkeit', in: *Gesammelte Schriften I.2: Abhandlungen* (eds. Rolf Tiedemann and Hermann Schweppenhäuser), Frankurt am Main, Suhrkamp, 1991, p. 491. English translation from: http://web.bentley.edu/empl/c/rcrooks/toolbox/common_knowledge/general_communication/benjamin.html

embraced the doppelgänger motif and related film to mirrors: in *Student of Prague* (1913), a man's life is taken over by his mirror image, which has become autonomous and three-dimensional, and murderous.

The video art of the past fifteen years, in which multiple projection has become such a commonplace, is itself a split doppelgänger of cinema; video art constantly reflects on the heritage of cinema, de- and reconstructing moments from film history. In *Confessions of a Justified Sinner* (1995/96), Douglas Gordon has staged the return of the gothic horror tradition and its filmic afterlife as a double projection in a gallery space. The two projections show slow-motion sequences, on one screen in positive and the other in negative, from the 1931 film version of *Dr. Jekyll and Mr. Hyde*, showing the transformation of Jekyll into Hyde and back again. The work's title refers to an earlier Scottish doppelgänger story, James Hogg's *The Private Memoirs and Confessions of a Justified Sinner*, 1824. Here, the relation of one image to the other becomes predicated on the model of the doppelgänger: the doubling of the image does not lead either to the aleatory effects of an 'open work of art' or to a dialectical montage in which images comment upon another; rather, the doubling of the image becomes an uncanny splitting and doubling of the allegedly autonomous subject, which no longer controls its own life. Rudelius too works with certain elements from the gothic tradition, but her montage practice aims to go beyond gothic dread. In both *Tagged* and *Economic Primacy*, Rudelius' precise, sometimes acerbic observations of both group behaviour and individual idiosyncrasies within larger social patterns show man as mass man, as a reproduction of certain sartorial and behavioural

7 Marcel Duchamp decribed the bachelor apparatus of his *Large Glass*, with its nine malic moulds, as a 'cemetery of uniforms or liveries'. See Marcel Duchamp, 'The Green Box', in: *The Writings of Marcel Duchamp* (eds. Michel Sanouillet and Elmer Peterson), New York, Da Capo, 1989, p. 51.

conventions; the doppelgänger is no exceptional phenomenon that inspires gothic dread, but commonplace.

Although the people in the films are quite at peace with their readymade selves and feel comfortable in their uniforms and liveries, watching them move and talk generates a kind of democratized, diluted sense of uncanniness.[7] Contrary to many *monteurs*, from Eisenstein to Farocki, who use montage of different images to shatter the circle of uncanny reproduction of sameness and introduce dialectical movement into the world of mechanical reproduction, Rudelius plunges into sameness. The young men in *Tagged* — most of whom still live with their parents — often spend their entire salary on clothes, and list the prices of the various items as they dress and undress themselves. They know the symbolical and monetary values of different brands, although the branded differences between the brands could be regarded as no more than a consumerist fiction. But *Tagged* and *Economic Primacy* also contain faint glimmerings of hope. Rudelius employs multiple projections — with their combination of diachronic and synchronic montage — to generate an open-ended dialectic between images and voices that are almost, but not quite, identical: there are differences, however minimal they may be. Although she came close with *Plush*, Rudelius is — thankfully — no Vanessa Beecroft, whose performers are dressed and made up to look like perfect clones. While the men in *Economic Primacy* are staggeringly alike in their ideology (anti-welfare, pro-'free market', and so on) and in their general appearance, they also perform their role in the symbolic order with intriguingly different accents. Often, one of the men seems to listen to what the speaker in the other projection is saying. As the non sequiturs, contradictions

and empty repetitions in their various discourses
accumulate, there seems to be a silent debate — a
possible debate — that is suggested by the editing.

In *Tagged*, there are recurrent images of boys
looking at themselves in a mirror. At one such moment, the projections on the left and right go black
— as the images in both works sometimes do, leading
to a kind of negative montage of images and black
(but subtitled) voids. In this particular instance,
the central image shows one of the guys looking into
the mirror, as he mentions that he checks whether
his hair and clothes are okay whenever he is near a
mirror. This moment of intense narcissism needs no
other image, as the montage is internal in the image:
the mirror doubling the boy within one shot (even
if we see only the reflection, the boy is present by
implication). However, towards the end of the shot
the boy looks distracted and blank. Perhaps this is
a kind of re-enactment of the mirror stage, in which
he is experiencing a budding sense of non-identity
between his self-image and his mirror image — and
between himself and the near-doubles among his
peers. In general, the small idiosyncrasies of the
boys and men in Rudelius' works, the minimal and
largely unintentional, uncoded, non-branded differences between them, suggest that doubles may contain
potential difference, that they may be able to differ
from their hypothetical model and break their mould.

The branded differences between fashionable
clothes in *Tagged* recall the equally coded differences between those even classier commodities: works
of contemporary art. The distinctions between artists
and their oeuvres could be seen as so many simula-
tions of difference, diligently staged by galleries
and their little helpers in art criticism. Like any

catalogue essay, this text too cannot help functioning on the level of advertising copy; comparisons between works by Rudelius and established artists like Farocki, Warhol or Dijkstra inevitably serve to legitimize the younger artist's work. This mechanism is crucial to writing about contemporary art, and it comes as no surprise that a gallery which prides itself on only showing 'historically important art' should explicitly instruct a critic writing a catalogue essay for one of their shows to compare the work of the artist in question to Bruce Nauman, in order to provide him with a suitably impressive pedigree.[8] Although the game is now being played with a neo-liberal fervour that would upset old-fashioned aesthetes and genteel art historians à la Wölfflin, they were always glad to put their art-historical connoisseurship and scholarly expertise at the service of the art market; contemporary critics – often with art-historical training – merely continue an established practice. However, refusing to compare one artist to another because this plays into the hands of the market is not a serious option. Rather, critical comparisons must serve an analysis that goes beyond connoisseurship or art-historical blackmail – even if it does contain elements of these. With its questioning montages of apparent sameness and possible difference, Rudelius' work is not the worst model for such an approach.

8 This happened to a colleague of mine; usually the comparative imperative is implied rather than pronounced with such explicit bluntness.

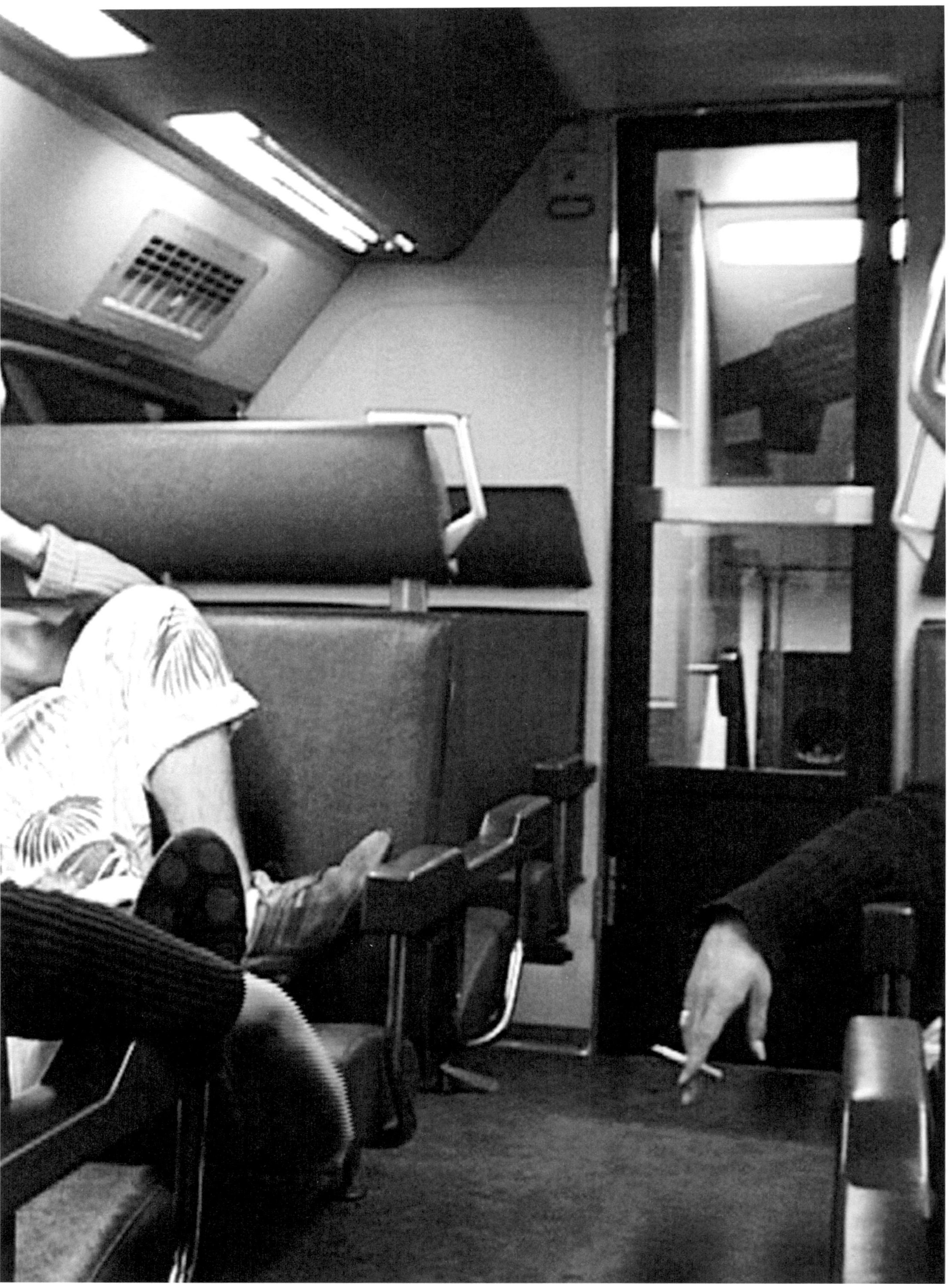

Read page 28

TRAIN

Video projection, 6:20
min, dvd, subtitled,
2001

With: Balder, Dan,
Rogier and Jan-Willem
(a.k.a. Nicholas)

Camera: Helle Lyshøj,
Julika Rudelius
Editing: Julika Rudelius
Editorial advice: Mark
Bain
Subtitles: Erik Pezarro

Funded by:
Impakt Festival,
Utrecht

TRAIN

VIDEO PROJECTION
6:20 MIN
DVD
SUBTITLED
2001

Train compartment at night, illuminated by neon light. The dark red plastic seats face one another in groups of two; they are the old-fashioned kind with a space in between the seat and the headrest. Four young men are occupying two adjoining groups of seats; they are smoking and drinking. Balder sits in the left foreground, Dan in the right foreground, Nicholas is facing Balder sitting in the left background and Rogier is facing Dan.

For the most part, only their mouths or the lower part of their faces can be seen, similar to how witnesses who want to remain anonymous are filmed. The cameras film from the seats behind them, through the gap between the seats and the headrests. The shots are mostly so close that only two men can be seen simultaneously. The man talk fast and loud, and they interrupt each other constantly. There is nobody else in the compartment. We hear the noise of the train in the background.

BALDER: Do you think Desiree's pretty?

DAN: She's got tits.

NICHOLAS: You know what?

DAN: She's a D. No shit.

NICHOLAS: She always wears a push-up.

DAN: The push-up makes her double D.

DAN: That's what they call her at work Desiree Double D. They do.

NICHOLAS: Who do you think is prettier?

ROGIER: Desiree.

DAN: Me too.

ROGIER: Natasha's fat.

DAN: Disgusting.

ROGIER: She's flabby.

ROGIER: You have to distinguish between women. Some women are only good for fucking. Admit it, it's true.* Some women... Like, Balder: and I met this chick yesterday. At the gym... She was really...

BALDER: Such a sweet girl.

ROGIER: She was a nice girl.

BALDER: A real honey.

ROGIER: I'd never use a girl like her.

DAN: Some women, you fuck 'em one night, and the next day you don't know 'em... That's the difference, some sluts... You chat them up and fuck them the same night.

*See page 23

You have to distinguish between women. Some women are only good for fucking. Admit it, it's true.

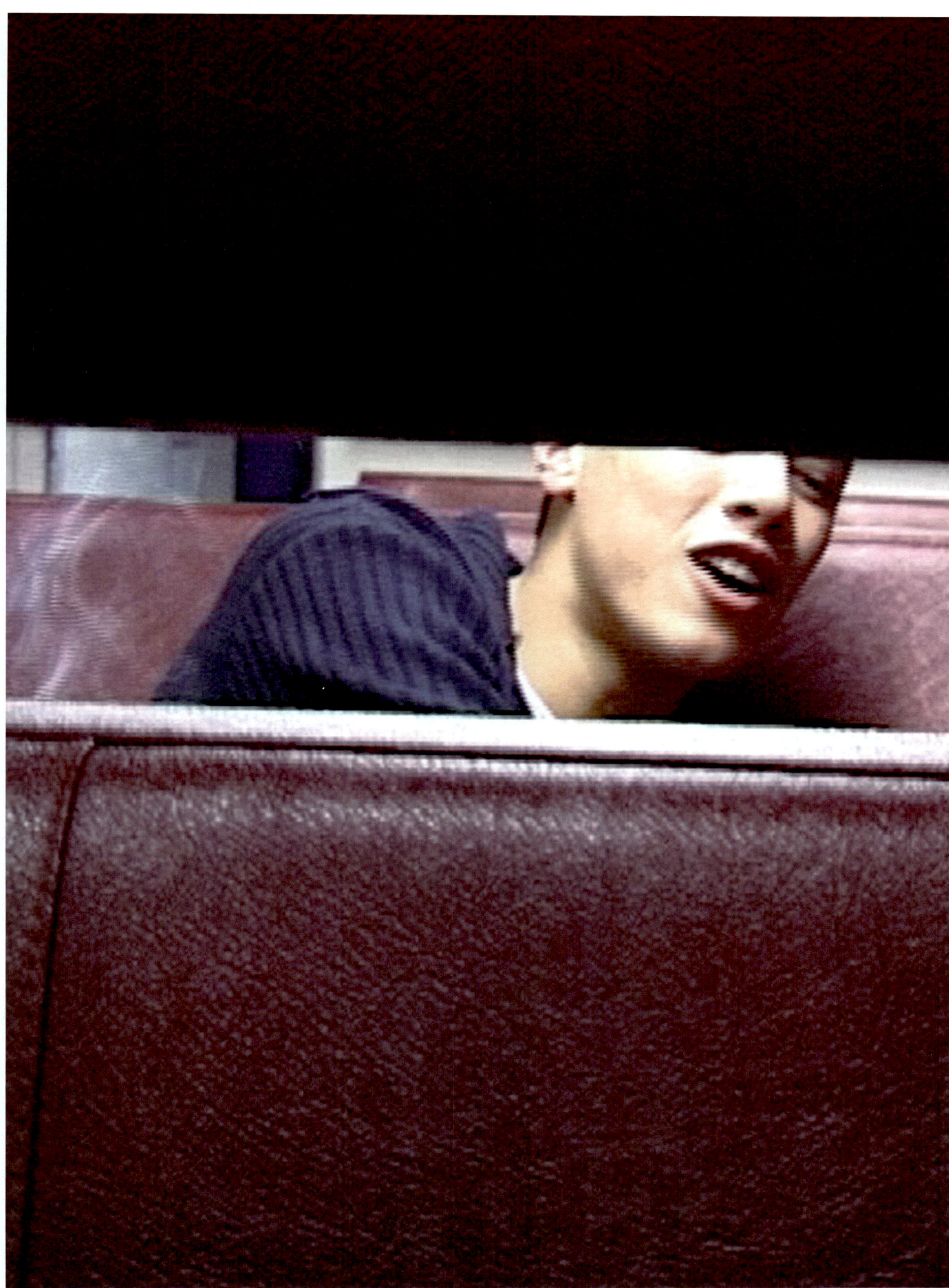

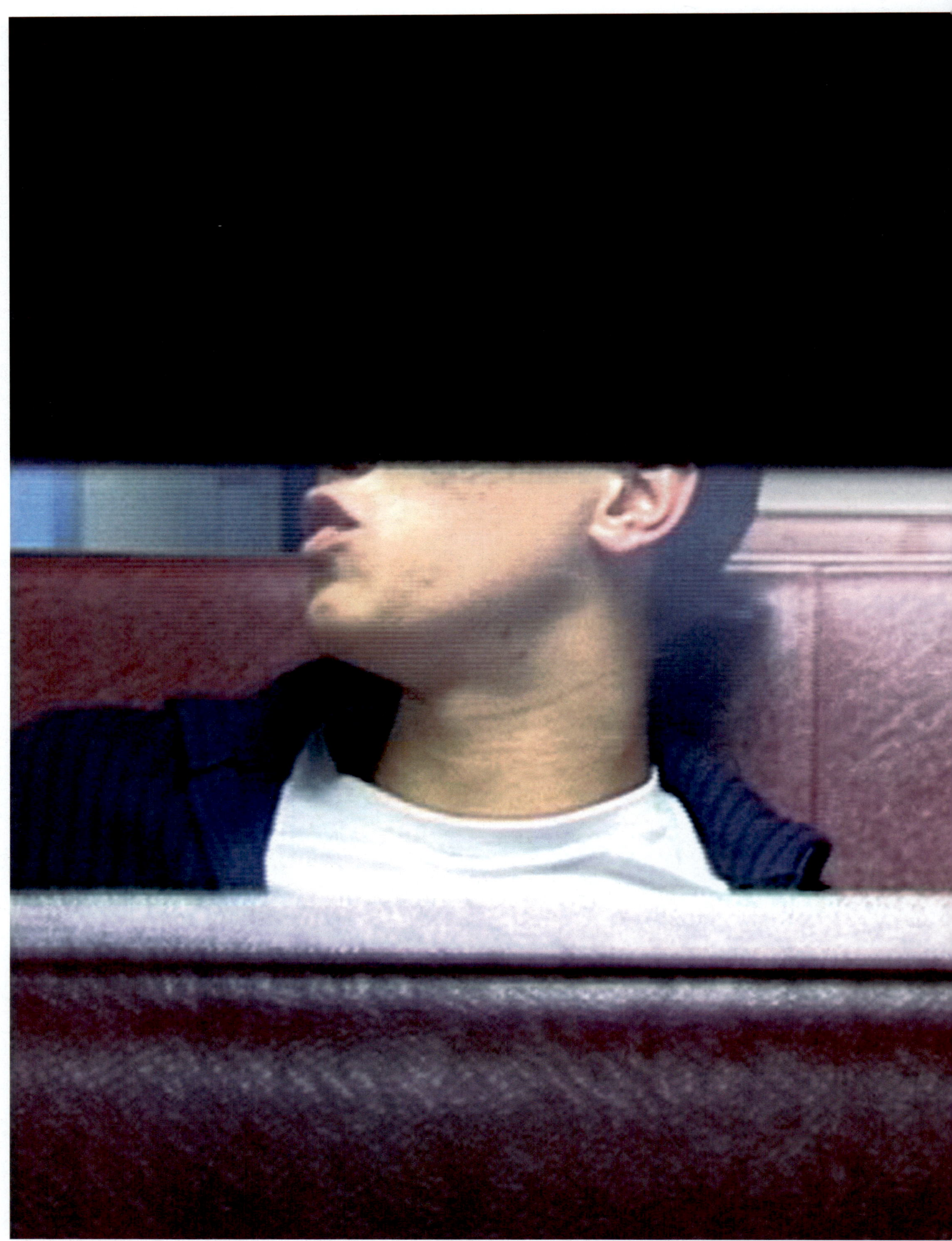

Read page 27

She's like the local 7-Eleven. Just give her a call. Can I drop by? You're open anyway.

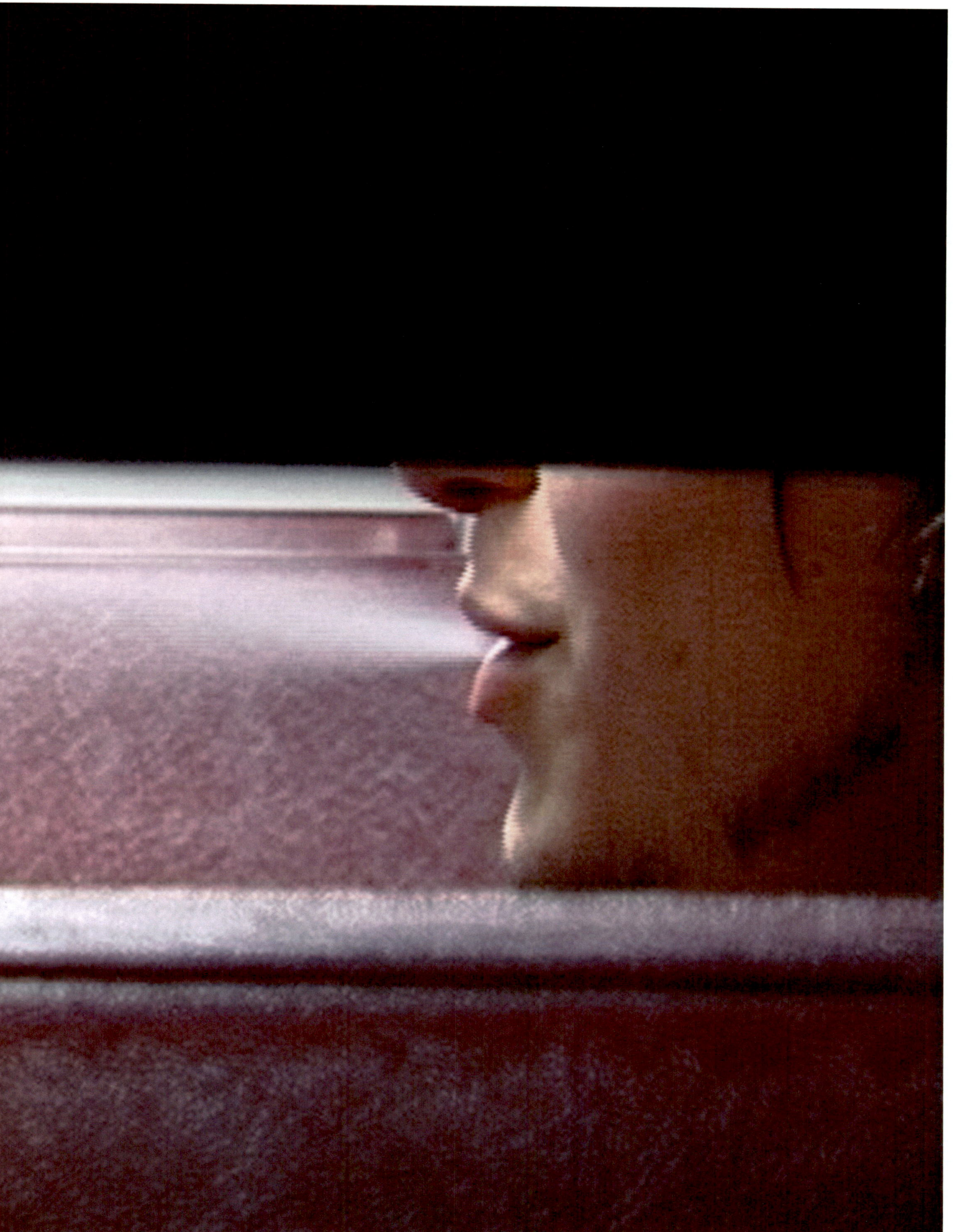

OK, call me a jerk if you like. But who do you blame the most? She's your girlfriend, but I'm a good friend.

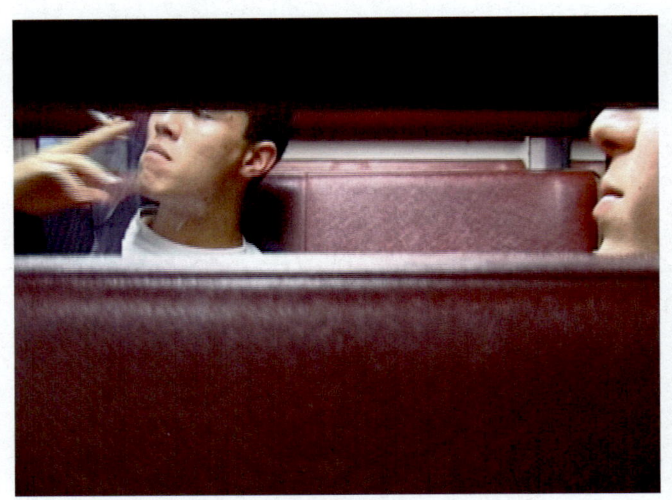
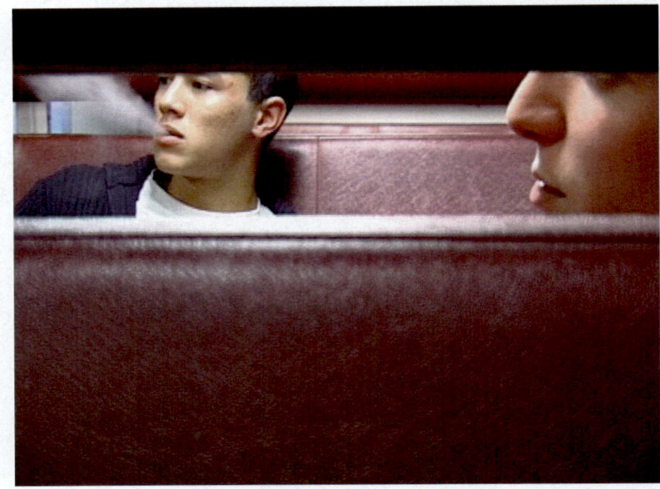
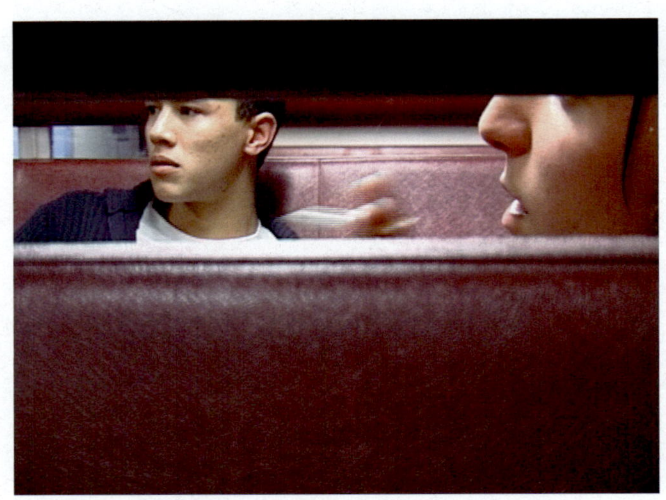
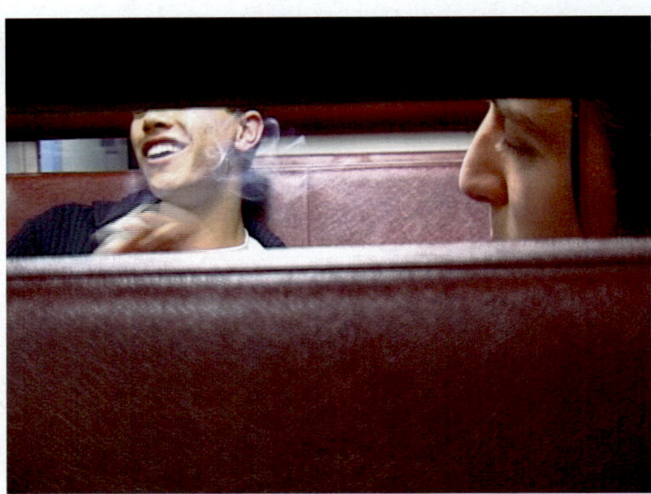
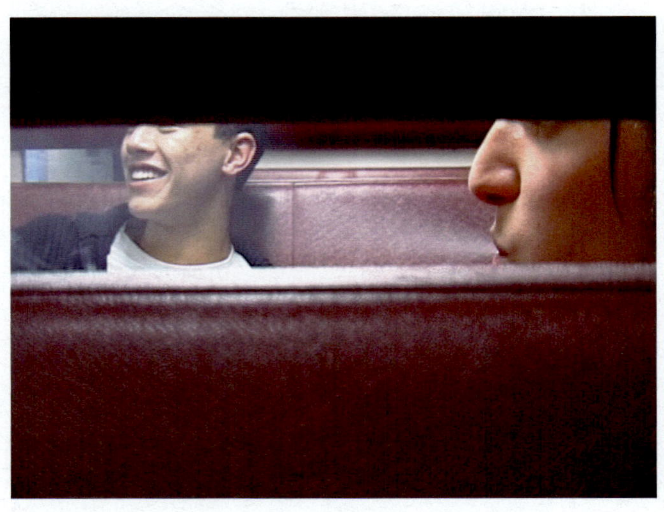
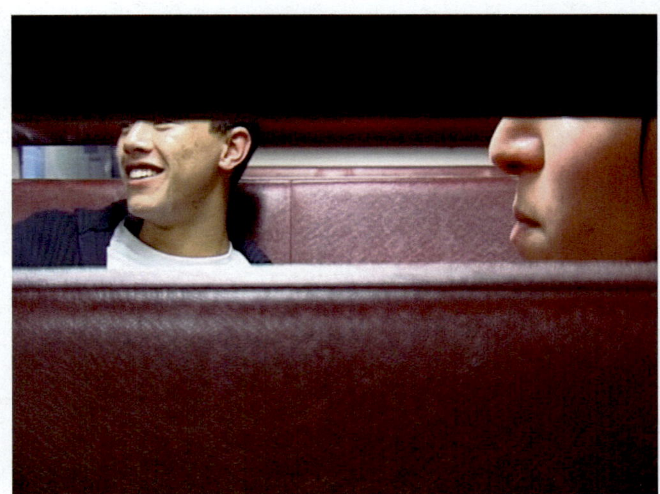

Read page 30

BALDER: You can spot that, when they're like that.
DAN: With women like that it's dead easy.
NICHOLAS: There's no challenge.
BALDER: What we did was disgusting. Well, what I did, I guess... It's a bit sick... It
           was her fault too. It was really disgusting.
ROGIER: But you're so easy.
BALDER: It was my fault too, that's true.
DAN: What?
BALDER: He screwed her on Friday afternoon and I screwed her Friday evening. I dropped
           by.
DAN: You stuck your dick in his cum.
BALDER: Yeah, really... But then again...
DAN: Brilliant!
ROGIER: She probably didn't tell you that we'd screwed that afternoon.
BALDER: Yeah, sure, I knew.
NICHOLAS: But did she tell you?
BALDER: I talk to him, don't I? He doesn't mind. I know you screw every Friday
           afternoon. So I called her on Friday evening. I needed somebody, and that was
           that... Really too slutty....
ROGIER: And my cum was already in there!
BALDER: Cycling home, I looked at my fly and thought, yuck, his cum is on my dick.
DAN: She's like the local 7-Eleven. Just give her a call. Can I drop by? You're
           open anyway.*
BALDER: On Saturday she was at Raoul's. Maybe Raoul fucked her too. If he did...
           that's way too slutty.
DAN: That would make it 3 guys in 30 hours.
NICHOLAS: I agree. Those girls are no challenge.
DAN: And they have no self-respect. With those chicks, you talk to them and fuck
           them on the first night. No self-respect... Sure, it's nice to satisfy your
           sexual needs. Just fuck her brains out.
BALDER: My guess is her cunt is all worn out.
ROGIER: No, she's got a nice pussy.
DAN: But it's still no challenge. Then the girl has no self-respect. Fucking two
           guys on the same night... OK, then she's a whore. It's way too easy, she'll
           get paid anyway... But Rose is different.

*See pages 24/25

BALDER: She should pay me.

DAN: She's different. I just don't get it.

ROGIER: But she has a crush on you.

BALDER: I can do what I like with her.

DAN: Who can't?

BALDER: No, really... How many times have you two shagged?

ROGIER: Three times.

BALDER: Without condoms?

ROGIER: She's on the pill.

DAN: So what?

ROGIER: OK, but fucking with condoms is a waste. I'm not used to it.

DAN: That's fine by me.

NICHOLAS: I've never done it with.

DAN: You've never even done it!

NICHOLAS: Course I have.

BALDER: Who've you done it with then?

NICHOLAS: Dorien.

BALDER: In your dreams. She says you didn't.

NICHOLAS: No, really. Listen.

BALDER: You going to tell that story again?

ROGIER: Let him tell his story. I wanna hear it.

NICHOLAS: I went with her after the party. 'Nicholas,' she said, 'You want to crash at
           my place?'... I said, 'Let's go to my place.' 'Yeah,' she said. 'Let's go to
           yours.'

DAN: To the point!

NICHOLAS: So we went to my place. We were in bed all night long. We didn't fuck. We did
           everything but fuck.

ROGIER: Did she suck you off too?

BALDER: She likes that. She sucked Frank Penders off in the playground. Fantastic. She
           loves giving head.*

NICHOLAS: On the swings!

DAN: She loves giving head.

NICHOLAS: I was sucked off seven times that night. Seven times, no kidding. No kidding.

ROGIER: Yeah?

DAN: You can't come that often.

*See page 20

NICHOLAS: But here's the point of my story: I didn't come once.
DAN: Shit, that's hell.
NICHOLAS: She kept stopping before I came.
DAN: Look, by then you're totally horny. Having your dick sucked seven times.
BALDER: Did you go down on her too? He got seven blowjobs and he didn't even lick her
           out!
NICHOLAS: That's OK. I have to be pleasured, not her.
DAN: The golden rule is, if she doesn't suck you off, you have to go down on her
           first.

Fade to black

DAN: The shitty thing is, it happened, and all I can say is I really liked her and
           I felt something for her. I thought, seize the day. I'll go with the flow.
BALDER: 'Seize the day.'
DAN: I'll seize the day and go with the flow. I was drunk. So was she. And she told
           me how she felt about you. It wasn't a big deal anymore. So I thought, 'Fuck
           it!' I wasn't planning on screwing her. But two weeks later it just happened.
BALDER: What? Did you fuck her too? When we were going out? Just tell me honestly.
           Just say what you did with her. That's so fucked up.
ROGIER: Why do you need to know?
BALDER: I just want to know. It's the kind of thing you want to know.
NICHOLAS: I think you should tell him the truth.
DAN: But I just told you the situation. These things happen.
BALDER: They don't just happen. You have to rule them out beforehand. That's bullshit,
           'These things happen.'
DAN: Did I start it? No.
BALDER: What? Did she?
DAN: I know that you...
BALDER: Don't tell me it's OK.
ROGIER: I know that Kay's your girlfriend.
BALDER: True, but that's over anyway.
DAN: I know you're together. I wouldn't chase her, even if I really liked her. I
           wouldn't say 'Let's get together? Kiss me...' I wouldn't say that. But she
           made the first move.

BALDER: It's finished anyway. I saw it coming. But it was still on then.

ROGIER: Just get rid of the bitch.

BALDER: Sure. One of my best friends...*

DAN: OK, call me a jerk if you like. But who do you blame the most? She's your
           girlfriend, but I'm a good friend.**

BALDER: It's just sick.

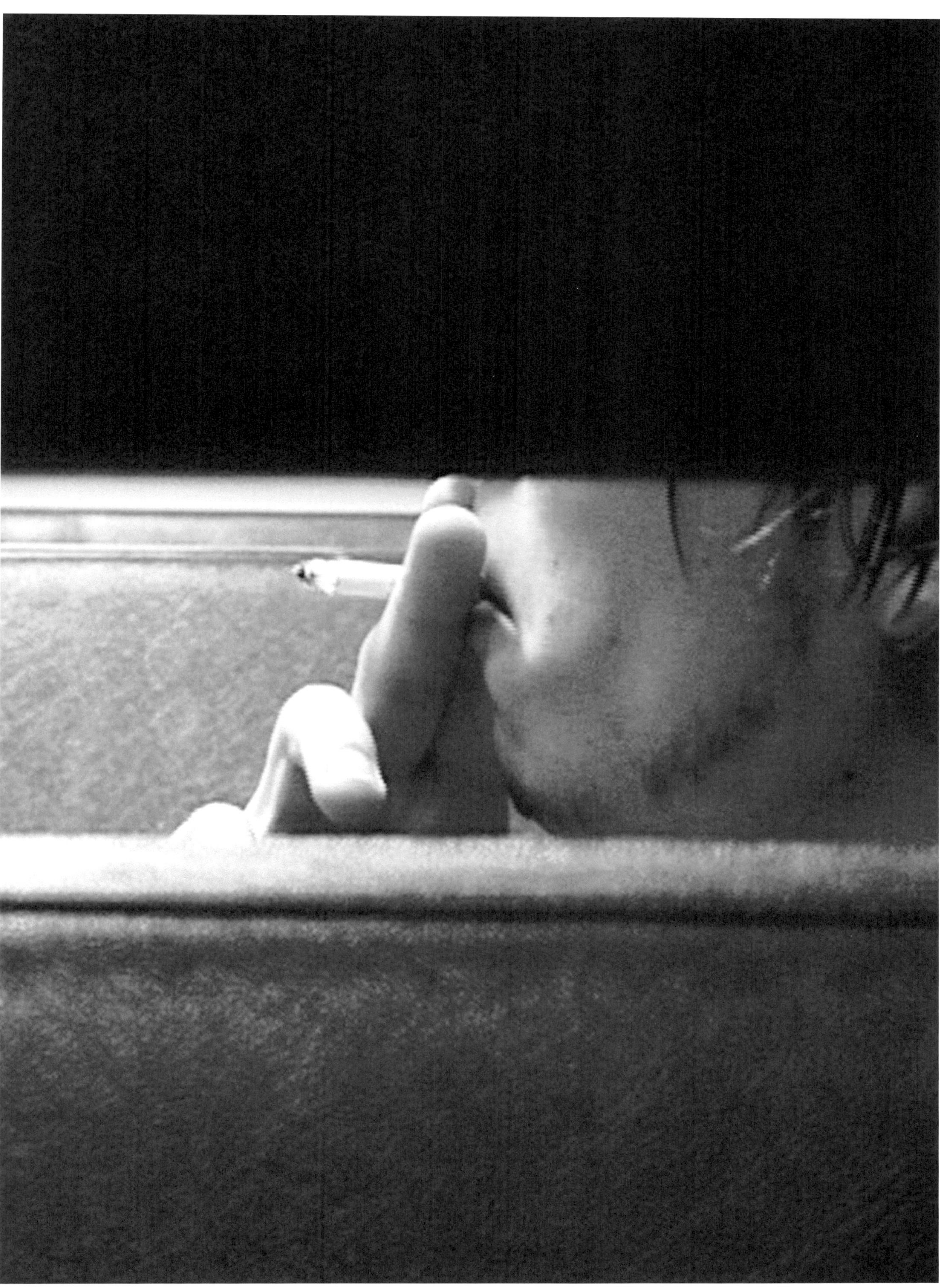

Read page 30

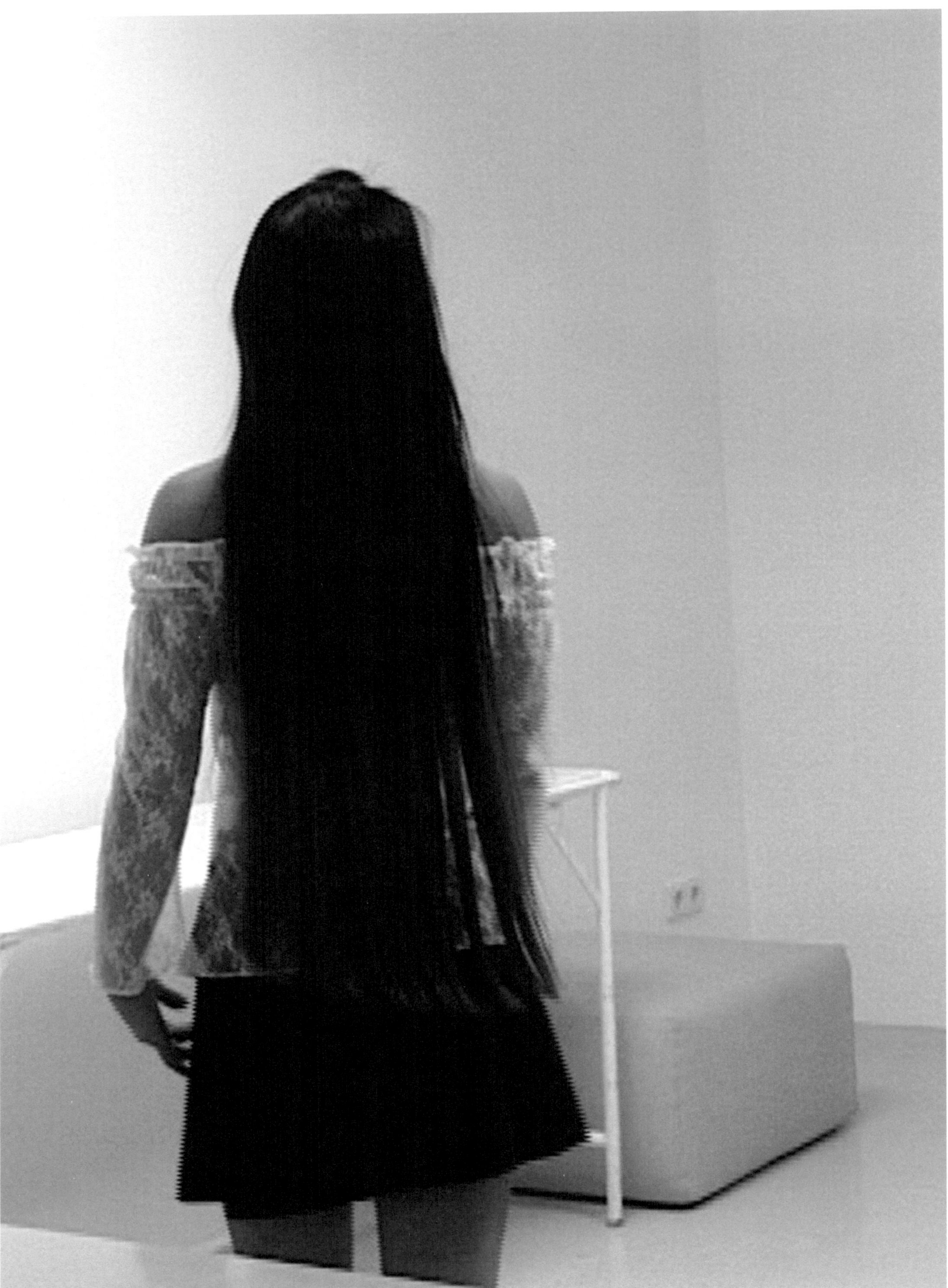

Read page 40

Video projection, 12:40
min, dvd, subtitled,
2002

<u>With</u>: Lena, Mieke,
Lucia, Manon, Esther
and Glenda

<u>Camera</u>: Helle Lyshøj,
Julika Rudelius
<u>Editing</u>: Julika Rudelius
<u>Editorial advice</u>: Mark
Bain, Marieken Verheyen
<u>Subtitles</u>: Erik Pezarro
<u>Location thanks to</u>:
Marty Lamers and Lucas
Ossendrijver

- 33 -

THE HIGHEST POINT

VIDEO PROJECTION
12:40 min
DVD
SUBTITLED
2002

A clean, white, roomy designer apartment with windows from floor to ceiling on one wall, sparsely furnished with a Pastoe couch, several designer armchairs, a shag carpet, a TV, a living room table and four Ahrend chairs. Most movements are shown from two camera positions simultaneously. The women's faces from the eyes up are hardly visible in the frame.

<u>Lena, waist-long black hair, red sleeveless shirt, black miniskirt and black boots. She sits on the table swinging her legs back and forth, touching her hips and bare legs</u>

Lena: I don't masturbate. That doesn't bother me. I don't mind other people doing it...* I'm not even curious how it is, because I know how I feel when I do come. <u>Cut to Lena from behind.</u> No, I would never do that. Not even if someone wants to feel it. Like if my boyfriend asked me to do it to myself... No.

<u>Wide shot: 180-degree pan through the room. Esther, long, blond hair in a bun, jeans, purple sweater, bare feet, lies on the couch with her face turned towards the wall</u>

Esther: For me, an orgasm is very intimate. I often do it to myself. With some boyfriends, I couldn't come. Because you have to give yourself fully. I have a really nice boyfriend now and it goes much more smoothly, better and easier. <u>Close-up: she moves into a seated position.</u> So I think some day I will be able to come just from screwing. <u>Close-up: Esther laughs.</u> I don't know when, but it'll happen.

<u>Esther stands up and illustrates her description with gestures</u>

Esther: My boyfriend is my size. We kiss. He grabs my bottom. I like that... He's got a nice butt, so I grab him there too, then we push up against each other. He starts playing with my breasts. That feels good. Then we start to kiss. Mostly I lie down on my back first. <u>She lies down on the couch.</u> I like that because I can feel his penis nice and close to my vagina. That feels good. But I always get a bit bored in the missionary position. I always want to move as well. <u>She grinds her hips.</u> I get excited and start to fantasize.** What I really like, is to tell him: I want something else, go get the condom. He gets the condom and puts it on, making love the whole time. <u>She kneels in front of the couch, resting her arms on it.</u> Then generally I get beside the bed like this and he

*See page 38
**See pages 36/37

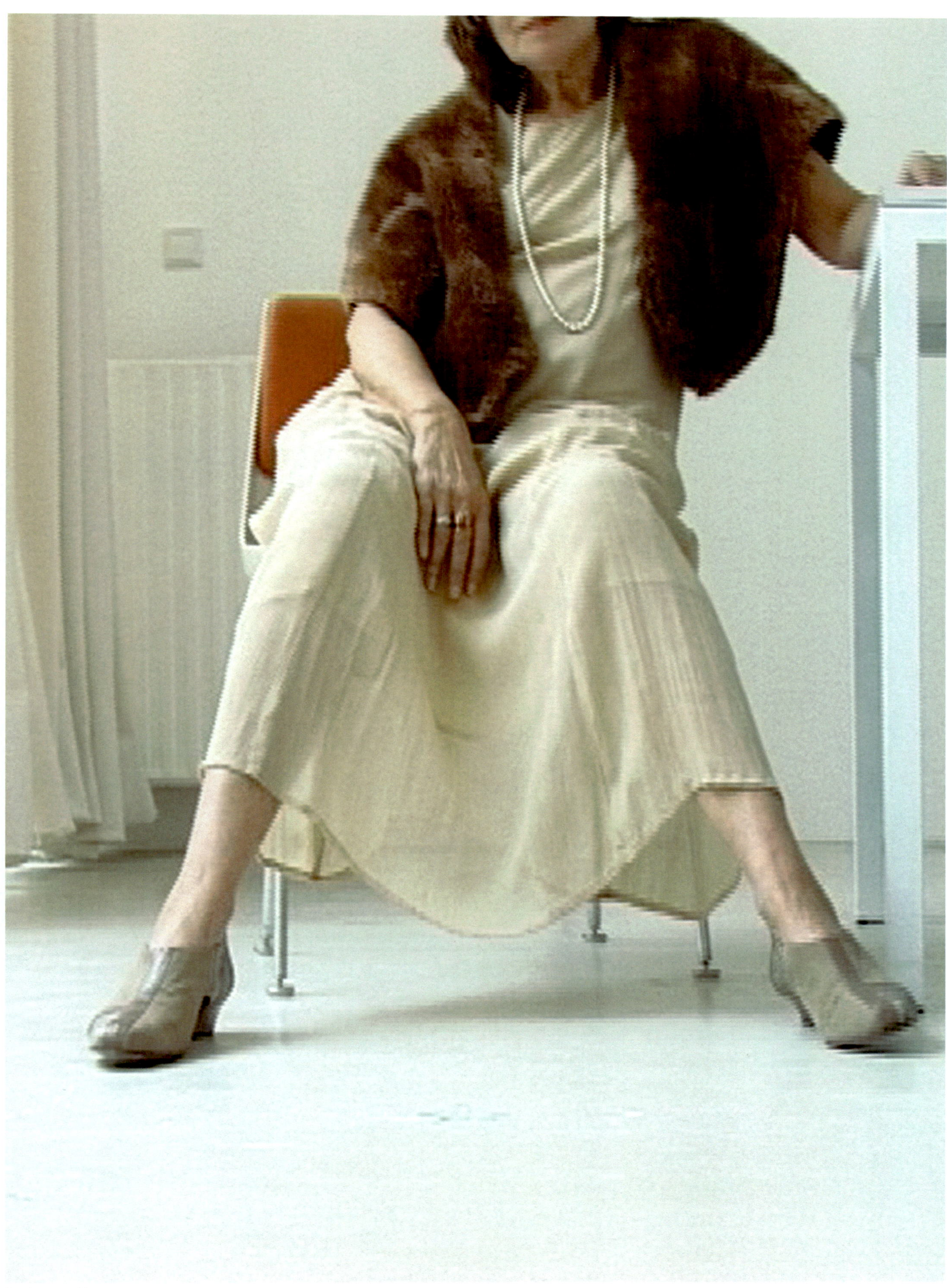

Read page 41

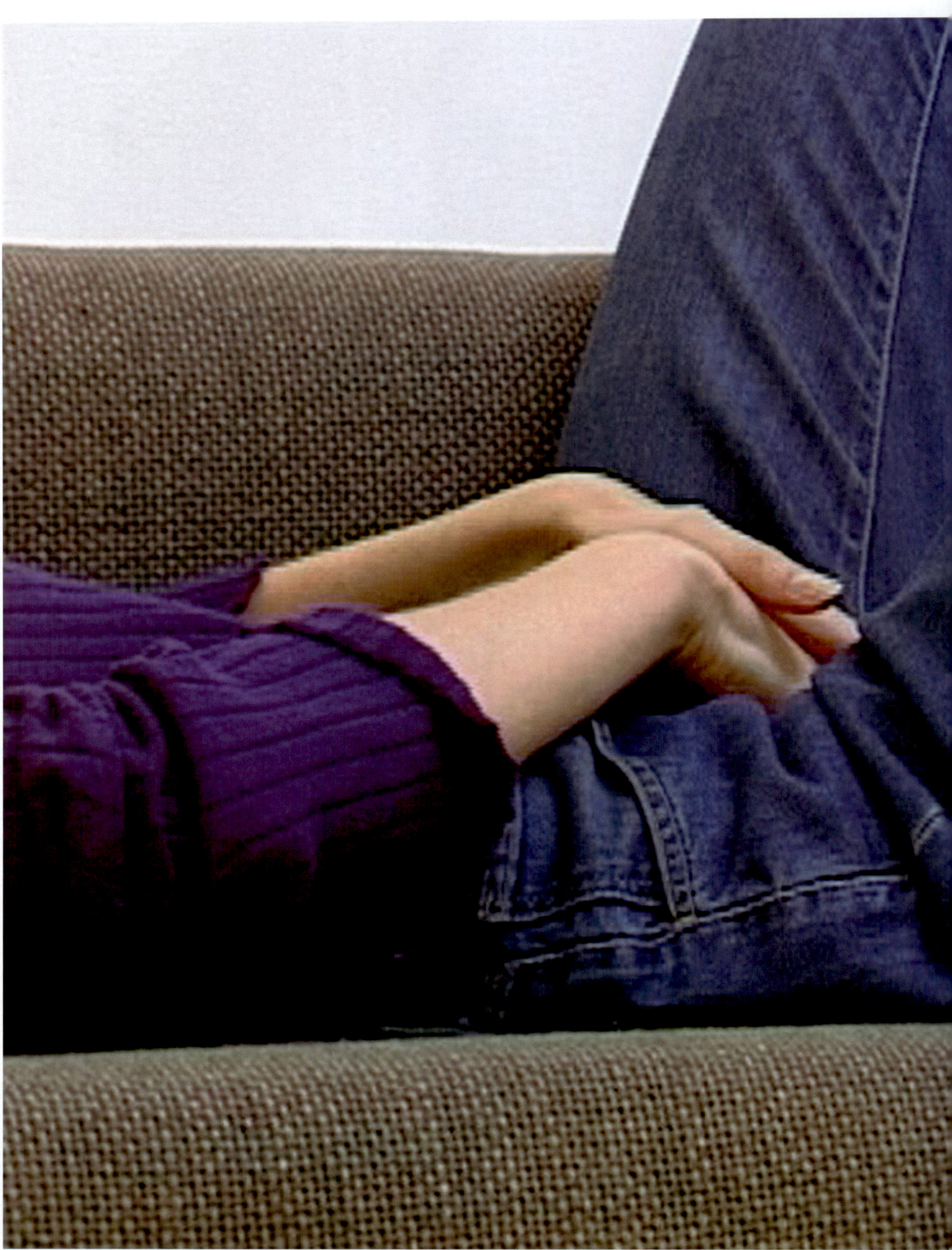

Read page 34

...I get excited and start to fantasize.

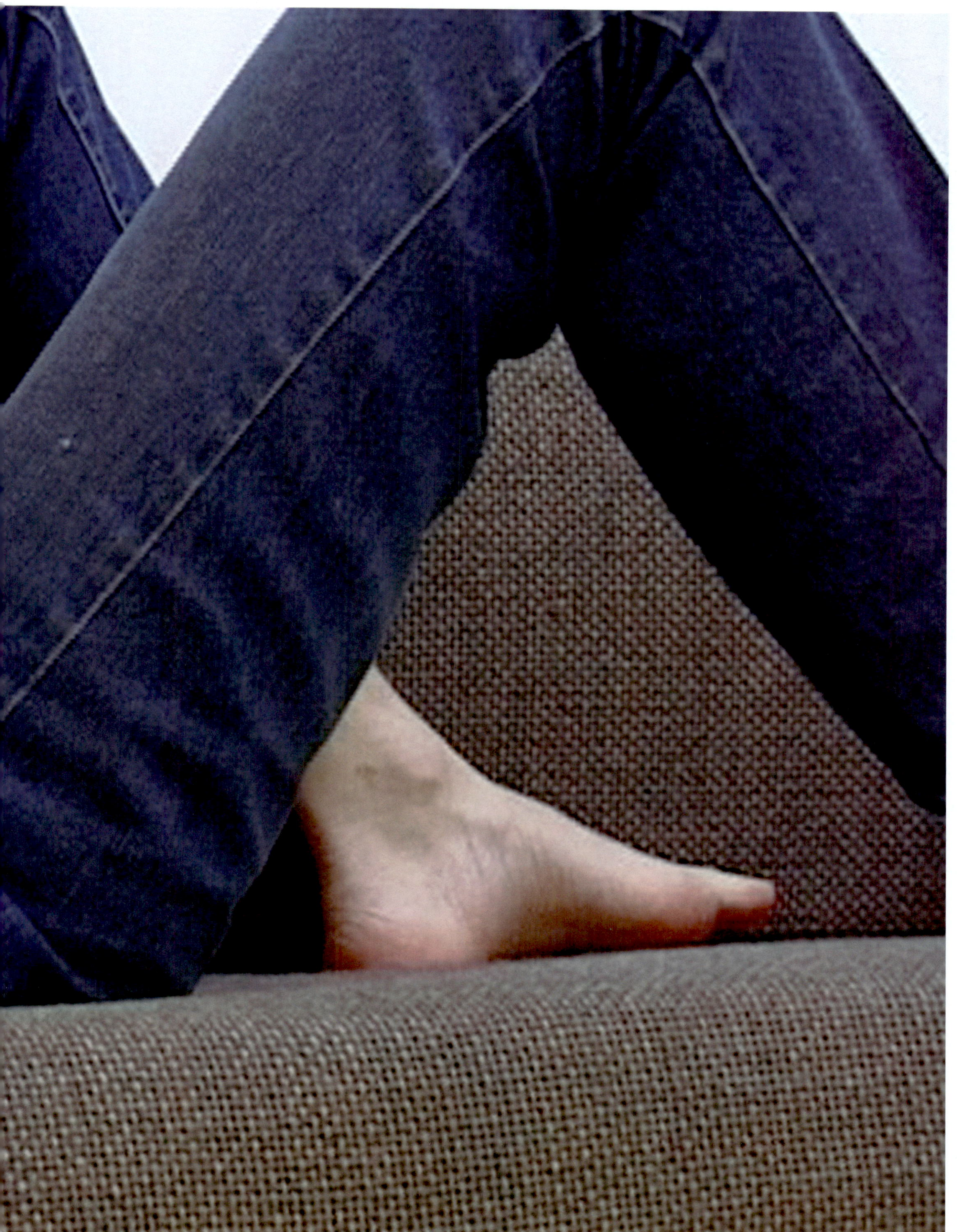

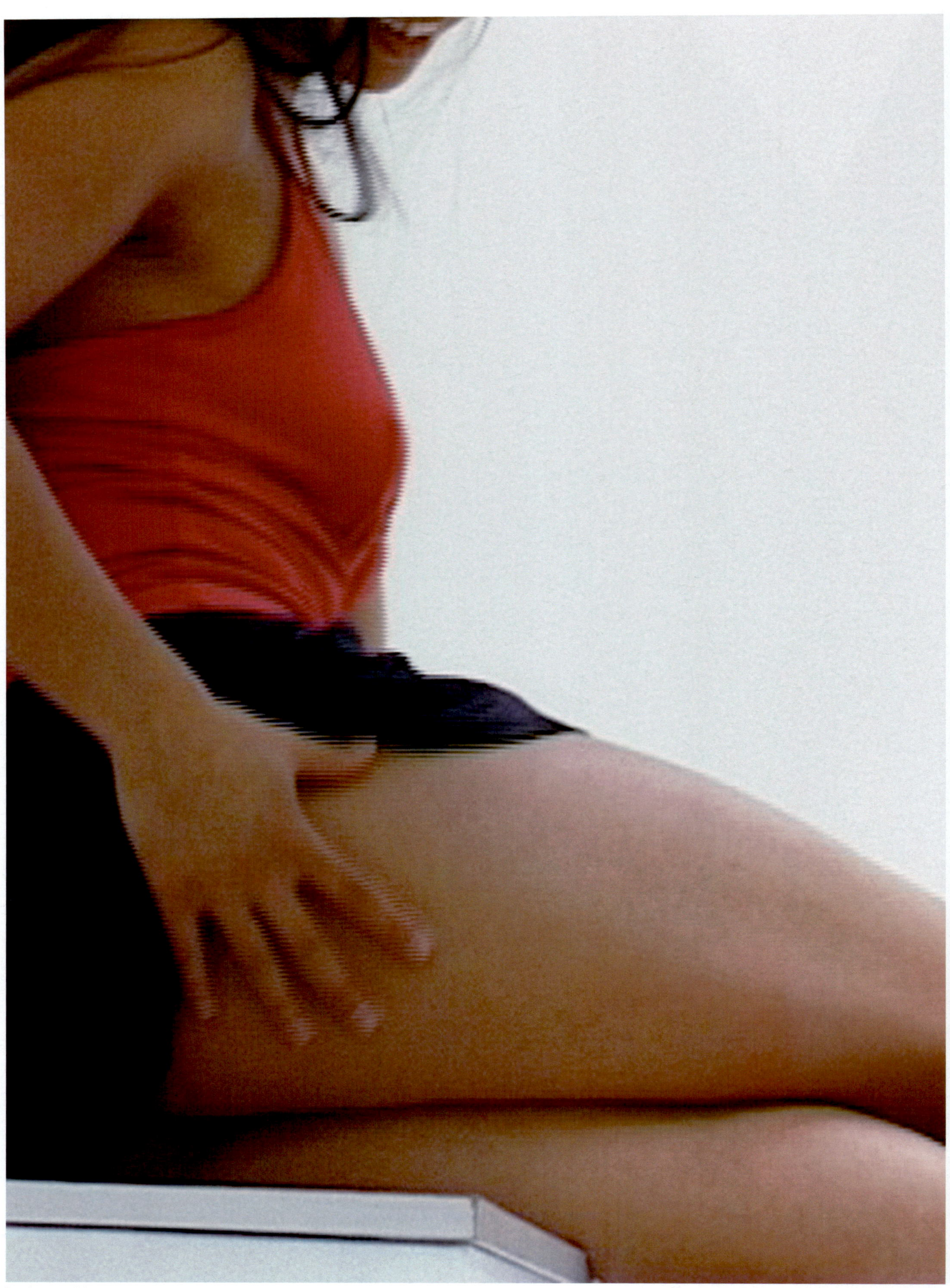

Read page 34

takes me from behind... That feels so good, giving myself to my boyfriend like that. I never did it with other boyfriends. It's nice because I can secretly finger myself. <u>Shot from behind, she rubs her fingers between her legs.</u> And he likes that too. Then we come at the same time. I love that. <u>She gets up onto her knees.</u> Then we've come and then we catch our breath and recover. He kisses me on the back. <u>She curls up on the carpet.</u> Then we lie down on the floor and cuddle up together and enjoy the afterglow.

<u>Close-up from above: Mariska, red skirt, red sun top, bare shoulders, brown curly hair. She sits on the carpet</u>

Mariska: Porno films can really turn me on. It's also a kind of laziness, when I'm not in the mood to come up with my own fantasies... while masturbating... when I'm alone at home, then I watch a movie. <u>She sits with her arms around her knees on the carpet.</u> Then, very gently I push one finger in. Usually it is very exciting when I feel that I'm very wet. Before I've even touched myself.
Very gently I move my finger back and forth. <u>She shows which parts of her hands she's using.</u> And I rest the palm of my hand on my clitoris, while one finger, usually my ring finger, is inside me. And fucking with my boyfriend I actually do it just the same way. When he's inside me. Often I'm sitting on him. Of course, my finger doesn't fit inside as well. I spread my fingers so that his penis fits between them. And I rest the palm of my hand on my clitoris again. Usually that gives me a really good orgasm. <u>Close-up from above.</u> But I can't come with just a penis inside me. I wish I could. I feel a lot. It feels really nice, especially when I'm very excited. But I really do need some pressure on my clitoris.

<u>Medium shot: Manon, full-figured, short brown hair, brown loose dress, high heels, fishnet stockings, moves her hips</u>

Manon: I love doing some nice sexy dancing up against him, bumping my cunt against his prick to make him horny, but to make myself horny too. I already am really. Yeah, I'm already wet. It's exciting. <u>Cut-away: Manon in stockings. She steps into her high heels.</u> And then I love riding him and turning it into a game. Dancing, moving my hips, like salsa dancing but with his prick inside me.

She lifts her dress, gets on her knees and places her hands in front of her. I sit on top of him and I put my hands down in front. Then I do this grinding playing with his prick inside me. Then you can just... She goes up and down. And up and down too. She gets up. And playing around a lot and stopping too and sometimes going really slowly. Close-up: her upper body with gesticulating hands. Eventually I feel like I can't hold off anymore. Then I start moving a lot faster. Then it really sprays out.

Wide-shot: the thin legs of a woman slowly walk onto the carpet

Manon sits on the back of a chair and illustrates with her hands as accurately as possible

Manon: Those ejaculatory orgasms I get from penetration. But the other kind, the ordinary ones, don't come from penetration... Unless I really hang over him, the way I just explained, really sitting on top of him so that my clit rubs up and down against his prick without really taking him inside me.

Lena makes some lap-dancing movements next to the living room table

Lena: Then I turn around and go like... Then I take his hand... and then he can go on and while I'm dancing, he can unwrap me.* Close-up from behind: she is pulling at her shirt. The first time I did it I thought, yuck, do I have to do this? I was a bit stiff really. But afterwards I felt like: I can finally do it. I've got it down pat.

Lena sits at the living room table. The tabletop horizontally divides the frame in two. She's wearing a black sweater, her naked bottom is in the shadow of the tabletop. She draws figures with her finger on the table

Lena: How I come? When a guy, very slowly, very sensually, makes love to me using his tongue to lick all over my body. Not forgetting my belly button... Yeah, with me it takes a lot longer before the climax finally comes... But he knows that, my boyfriend, that I don't come... But I don't mind that, because we just keep on going. We always keep on going after he's come... Sometimes he's tired.

*See page 32

She giggles. Too bad for him.

Lucia, semi-long reddish hair, long beige dress and a fur stole, sits on the edge of the living room table

Lucia: You can do it yourself, then I finger myself... You use your middle finger and you start gently caressing your body. It's always different... You might not touch your clitoris or you might touch it. Close-up: Lucia's legs as she scratches her ankles with her shoes. It depends on how excited you are. And together with a man I find it very exciting when his dick is only partly inside and I have room to play with my finger too. And after I've come he can go in all the way and fuck me hard. I really like that. She still sits on the edge of the table holding her knees in her arms, rocking back and forth. But everyone's different. A lot of men can't put it in a little bit. They can't wait. Or you can't get your hand in between. Lucia from behind, looking out onto the patio. But if I don't come, I don't like it. I won't have that.* I want to come, just like the man.

Manon stands next to an armchair, then she turns and throws her upper body over the back of the chair

Manon: Sometimes he pushes me against the wall and tries to put it in. That doesn't go so well... And other times he shoves me over the table like this and sticks it in from behind. She gets up again. That feels so amazingly good, to have him holding me by the hips and then he whams it in.

Mieke, thin, short black hair, jeans, black high-heeled boots, black top, walks quickly back and forth on the carpet. As she walks, she keeps her hands on her buttocks

Mieke: We go to bed, then there's physical contact and we have sex... She sits down in an armchair. It depends... If I come first, I always want to stop right away. She leans back. Then I've had enough. With her outstretched hands in front of her, she makes pressing movements towards her body. But when I realize I'm about to come, and he's inside me then I push his ass down and in. So he stays there... and then I come. She sits up. But if it takes too long and I don't feel like it anymore... and especially if he's already come, then we have to finish it off manually... Then I take his hand and think, now it's my turn. That's all... Then it doesn't take long.

<u>Close-up: Glenda, short brown hair, army trousers, purple velvet bodice. She sits on a small table leaning against the wall with one knee up, biting at her lip</u>

Glenda: She turns me over. That excites me... So that I can't use my hands. So that I can't do anything anymore. I stick my ass up in the air. So she can get to it better. She sticks in her fingers. Two, three, four... It depends on how it feels... Maybe a finger on my clit. Maybe a finger in my anus... With a little luck I'll come. Otherwise we try another position. Or we swap. So that I do her first...* What she likes most is to be eaten out. <u>She laughs, gets off the table and walks out of the frame.</u>

*See page 43

Or we swap. So that I do her first...

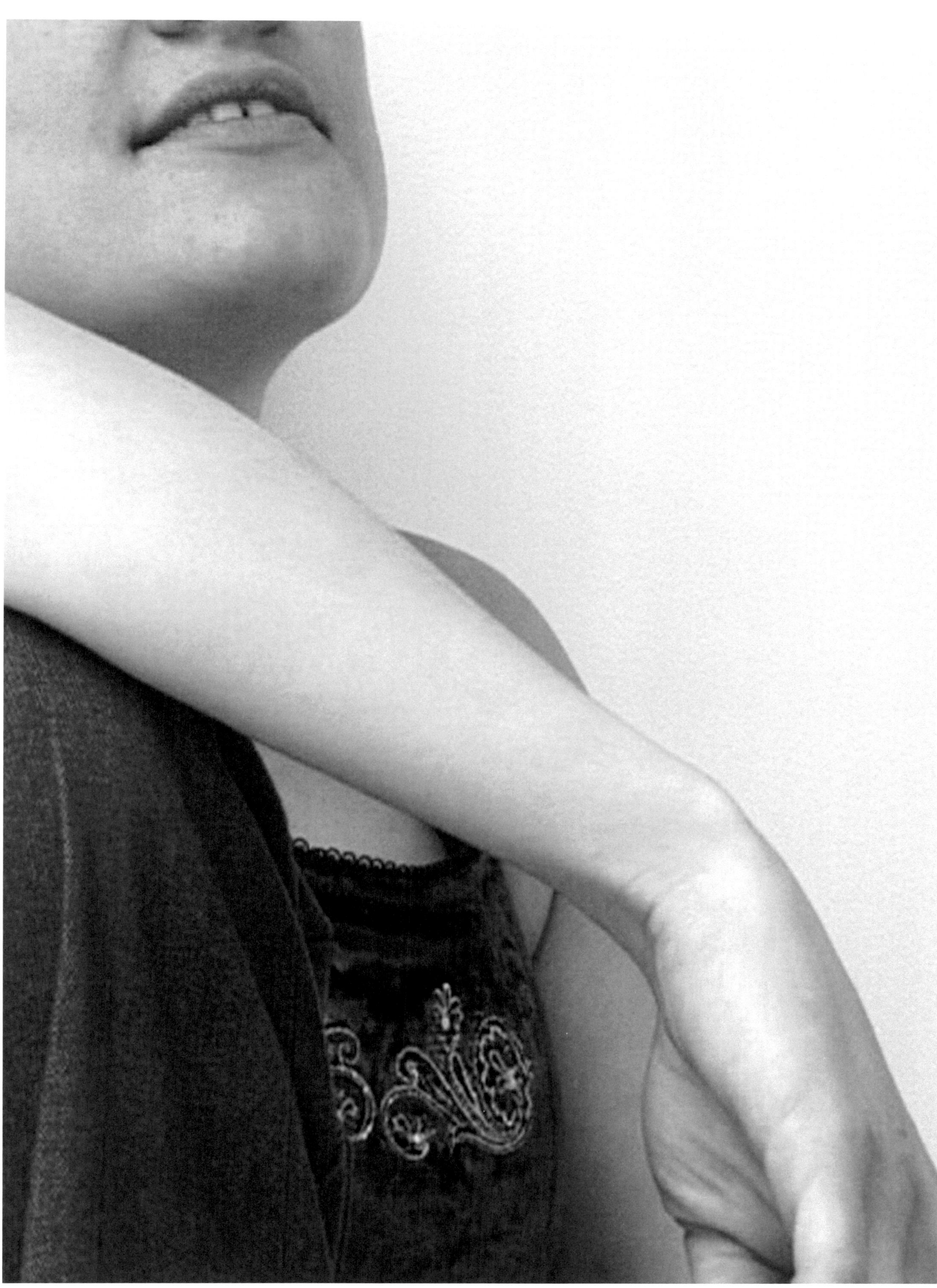

Read page 42

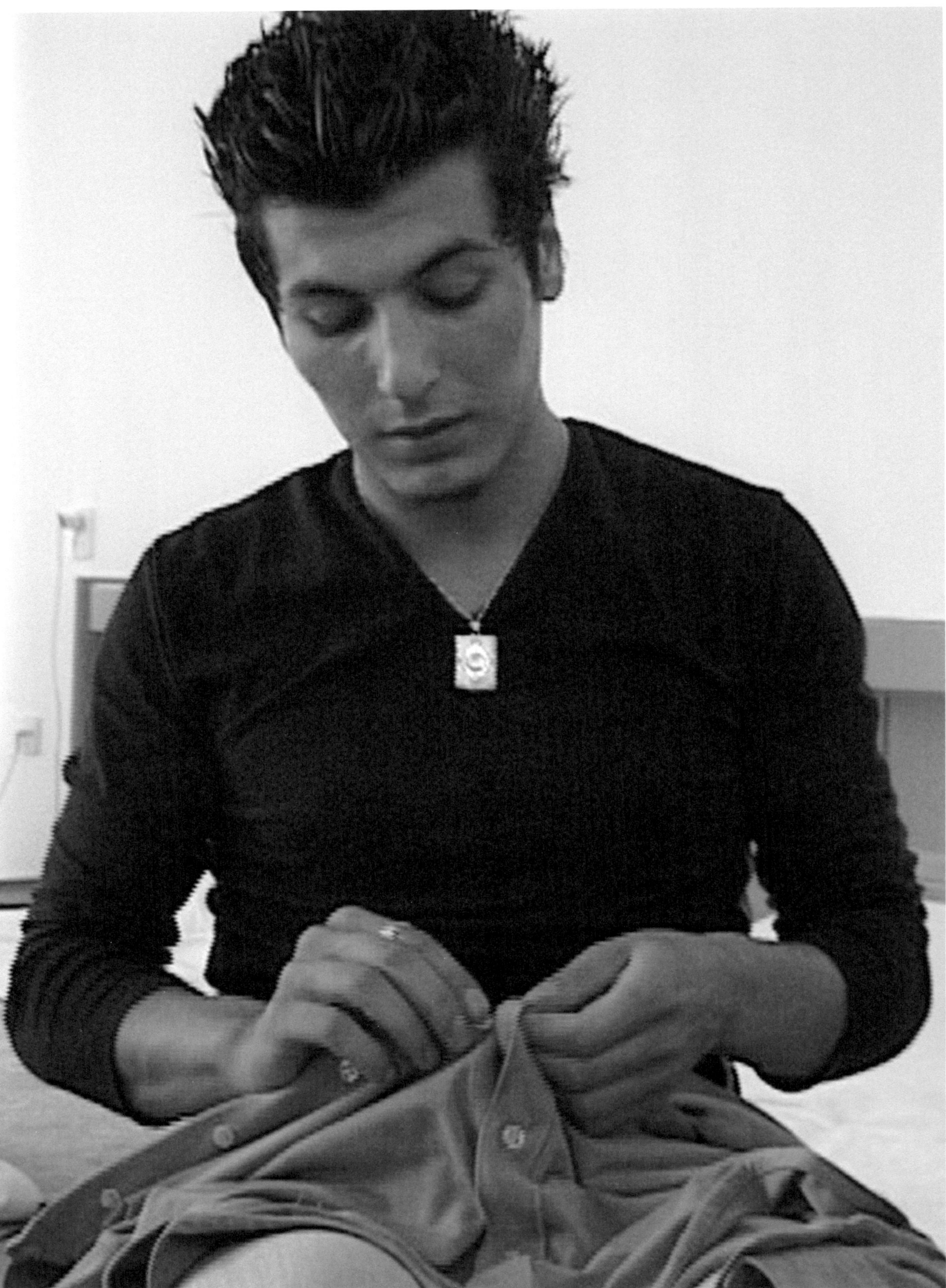

Read page 54

Video installation,
13:24 min, subtitled, 3
dvds, 2003

3 synchronized
projections, with
separate soundtracks
played via 6 speakers
which are placed on the
opposite wall from the
projection

With: Moussad, Grosjan,
Benny, Yamahal, Cuma
and Mutahir

Camera: Bert Oosterveld
Editing: Martin Hansen
Sound edit: Guy Amitai
Subtitles: Erik Pezarro
Assistant: Helle Lyshøj
Location thanks to:
Anuschka Blommers
Additional thanks to:
Marieken Verheyen,
Marty Lamers, Uta
Eisenreich and Thomas
van der Linde

Funded by:
Netherlands Foundation
for Visual Arts, Design
and Architecture,
Amsterdam

TAGGED

VIDEO INSTALLATION
13:24 MIN
3 DVDs
SUBTITLED
2003

An average hotel room, big, orange double bed, wardrobe and sideboard in birch veneer, which matches the colour of the bedspread, a dark wooden floor, opposite the wardrobe a row of windows with a beige curtain. Six young, good-looking men change clothes mostly in the space between the bed and the wardrobe, trying on different outfits and looking at themselves in the mirror next to the wardrobe.

LEFT SCREEN	CENTRE SCREEN	RIGHT SCREEN
		Moussad, early twenties, slender, curly black hair, white boxers, bare chest, puts on jeans
		MOUSSAD: These are Versace jeans. They cost about 180 euros. They were black. I bleached them. If you wear bleached jeans, they think they're cheap work jeans then you flash the label and they go quiet... Then they go: Oops! Sorry. I like to wear beautiful clothes. Not black every day... Every day, it's: I want more colour, more something that's really in fashion...
Close-up: Moussad's face in the mirror, looking at himself	Close-up: shorts being put on over black boxers	
Close-up: denim jacket being put on	Moussad tries on a summer hat in front of the mirror, then he takes his shirt off, but keeps the hat on	
Grosjan and Benny, both tall and muscular, hair long on top, shaved underneath. Grosjan has a goatee, black curls, Benny is clean-shaven with blond hair	MOUSSAD: ...that makes you look better. If your jeans are black, black sweater, black jeans, black shoes, black cap... On the street they think: He's a delinquent or that guy is up to something.	

You can't stay in the 80s, walking around in cowboy boots while the rest of the world moves on.

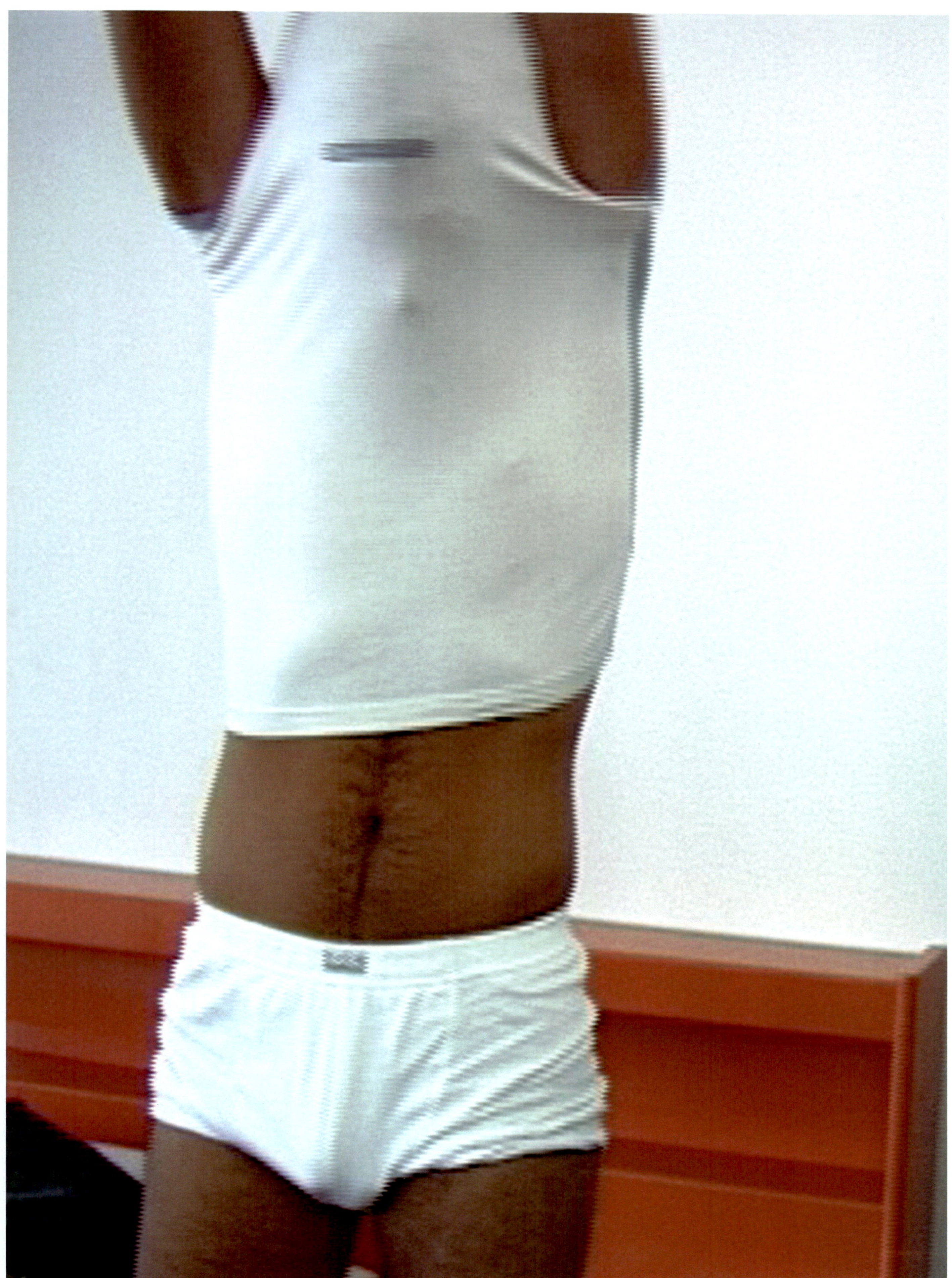

Read page 51

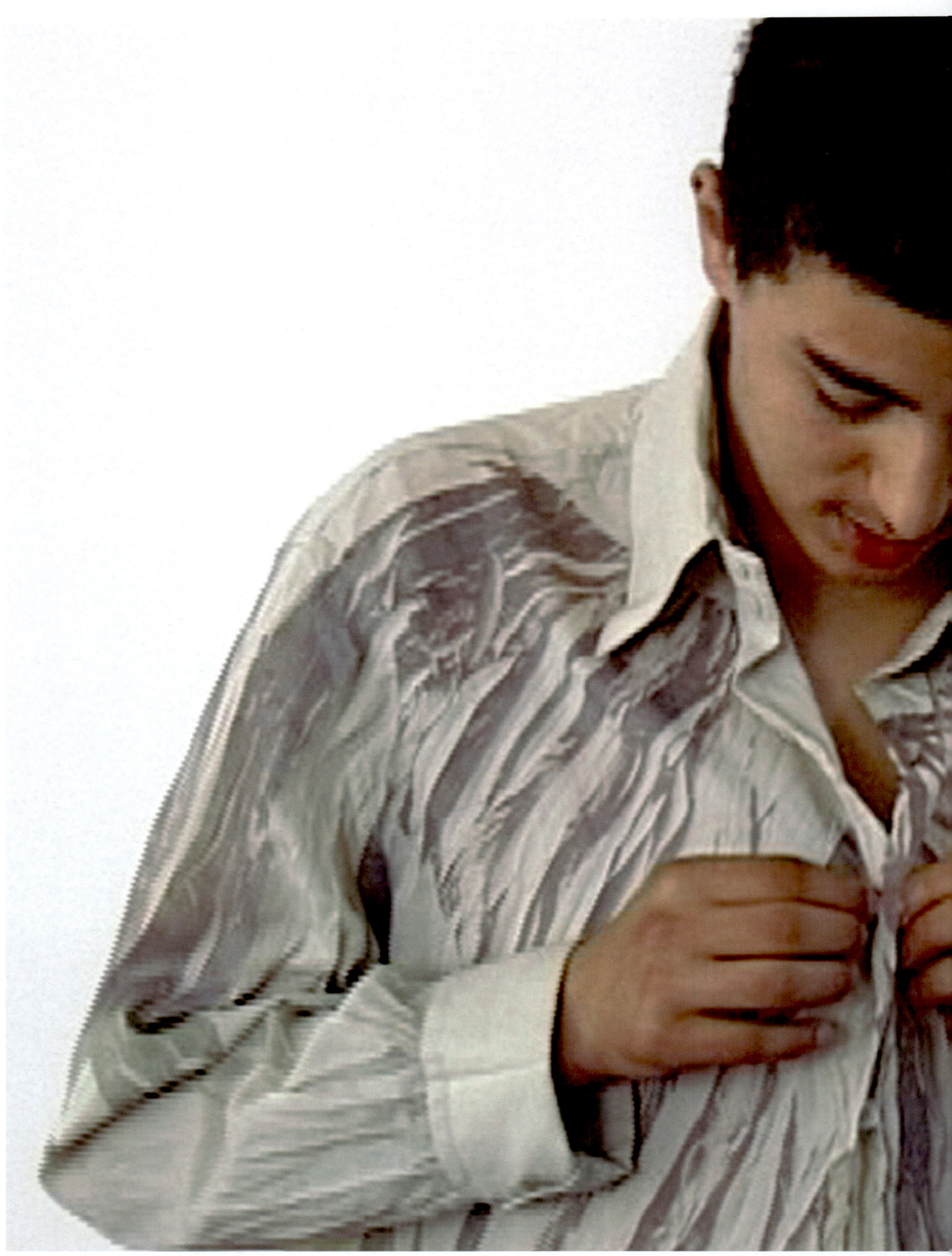

I want them to see me as a normal guy not someone who acts cool with his clothes...

Read page 54

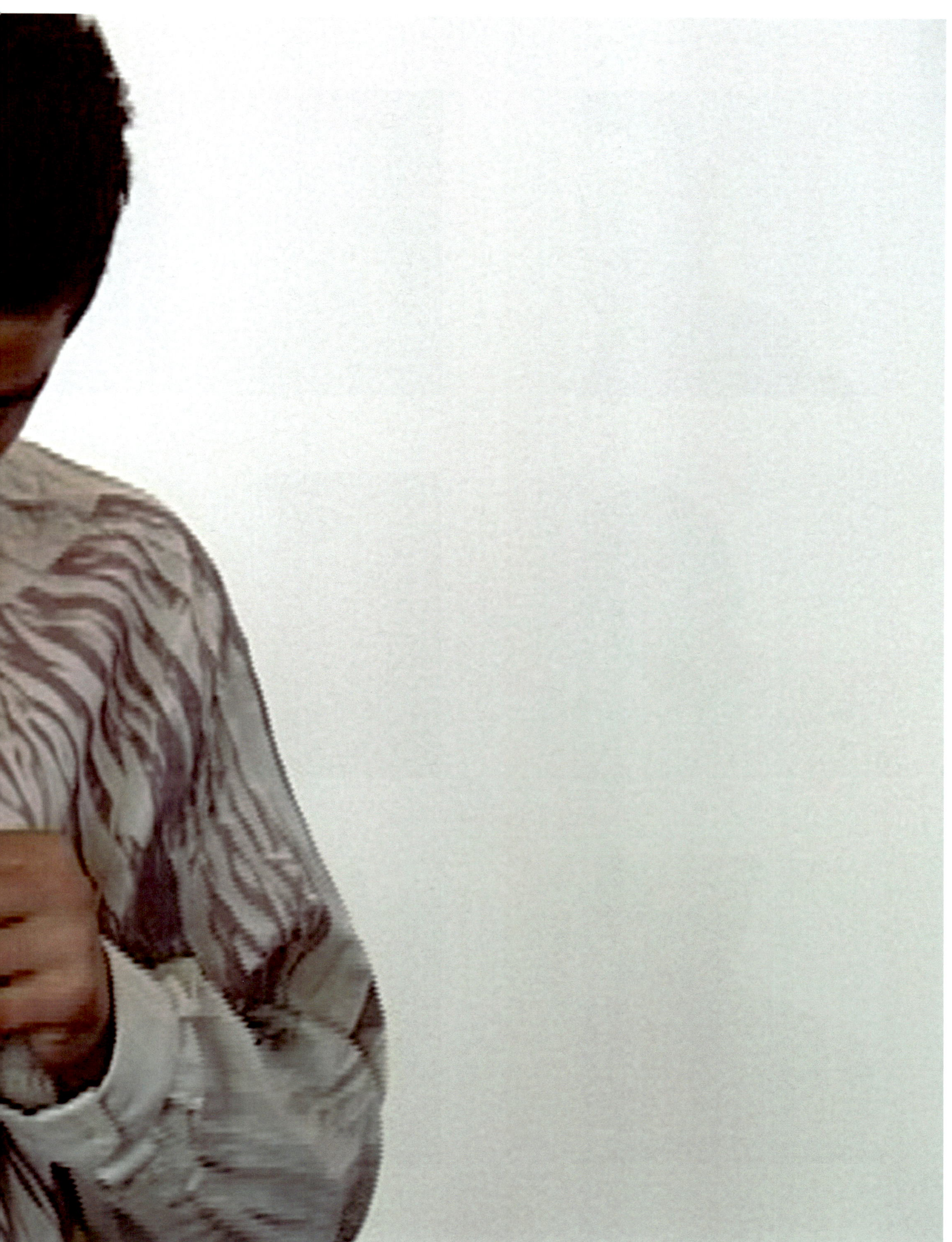

I think clothes come first. You have to look good. For yourself, so people can see you look good.
Then they respect you more. And you're cooler, of course.

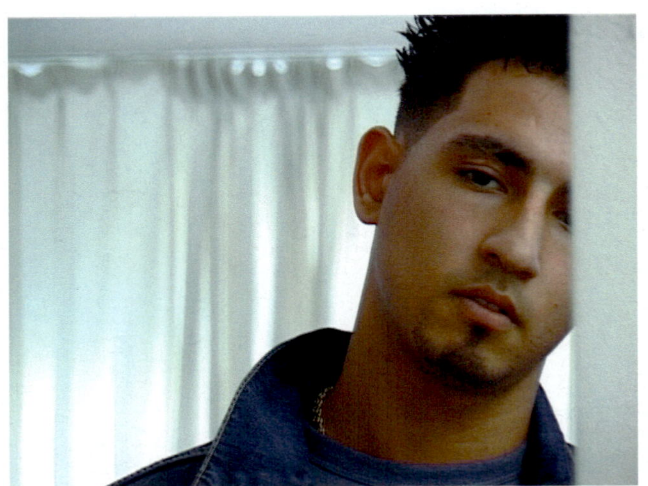
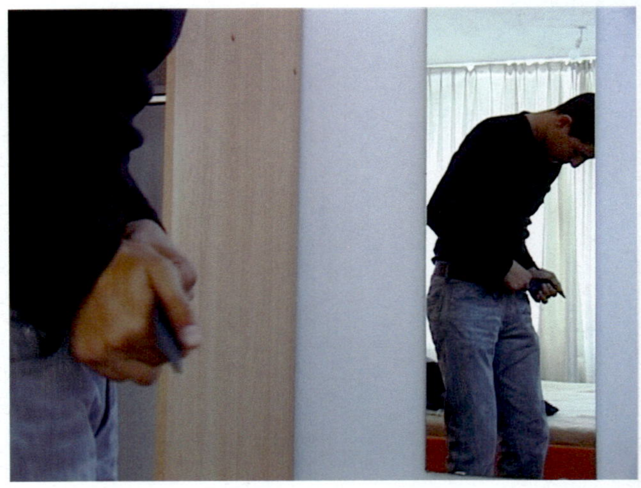

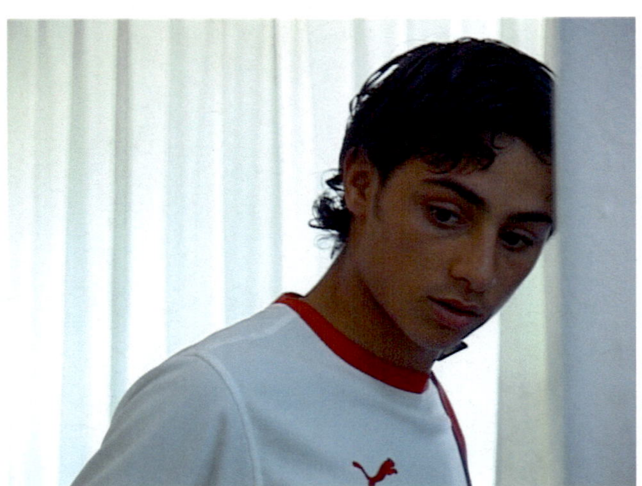
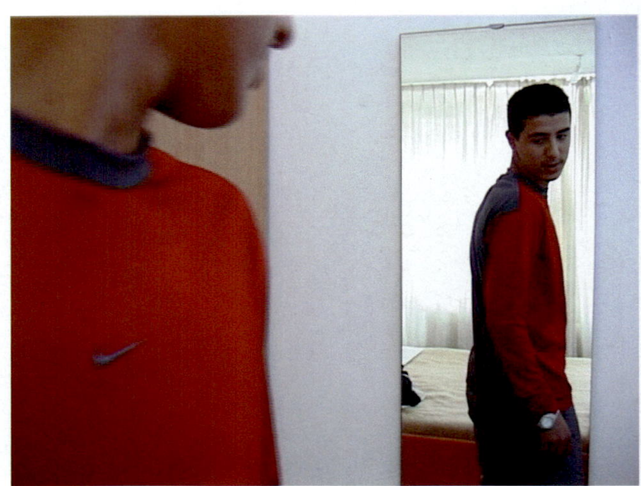

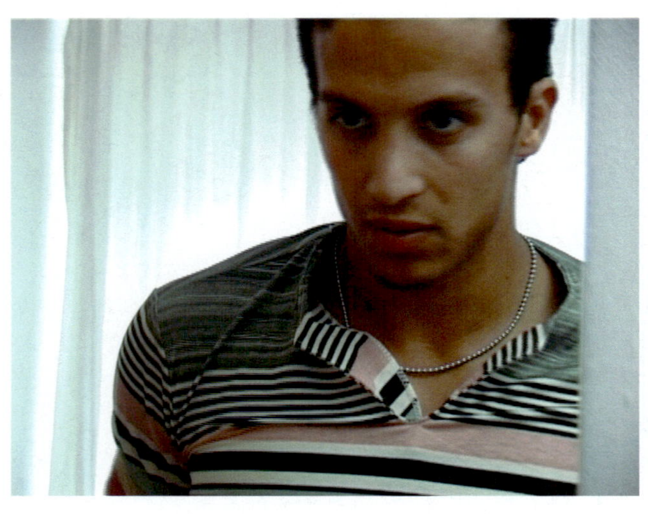
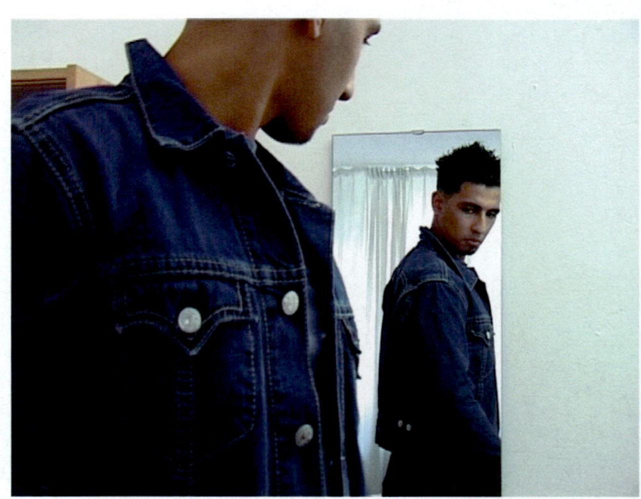

Read page 55

LEFT SCREEN   CENTRE SCREEN   RIGHT SCREEN

GROSJAN: If my girlfriend   Medium shot of bare legs
sees a guy the first thing   with hands removing Nike
she does is look at his   sandals, we hear the
shoes. People used to look   scratching sound of the
at faces. Where's he from?   Velcro
What's his background?
Zoom in on his face.   Close-up of a bare back:
What kind of... How's   a black shirt is being put
he look? Does it all go   on
together and look good?
But nowadays: Hey, are
those Pradas? H&M? Forget
it. Doesn't matter. C&A?   Close-up: Moussad's face**
Forget it.

                                   MOUSSAD: Then you show,
                                   kind of, that you're a
                                   somebody or... Sometimes
                                   you want to belong. Yeah,
Grosjan looks at himself   you've got that coat worth
in the mirror, arranges   500 euros. Honestly: I
his gold chain   was 15 when I bought that
                                   coat. I just wanted to
                                   belong. I worked hard for
                                   that coat. But it is good
Close-up: Grosjan's face   quality. It'll last.***

GROSJAN: You can't stay in   Moussad changes from a
the 80s, walking around   black shirt into a white
in cowboy boots while the   shirt   Benny puts on a white
rest of the world moves   T-shirt
on.* You can't. That   Bilal checks himself in
wouldn't be right.   the mirror   BENNY: This is Evisu. 150
                                                                   euros.
Grosjan bites his lip

LEFT SCREEN	CENTRE SCREEN	RIGHT SCREEN

LEFT SCREEN

Close-up: hands zipping pants up

MUTAHIR: This is Replay. 70 euros.

Benny puts on a T-shirt

BENNY: This is a Dolce & Gabbana T-shirt.

Benny looks down at himself

BENNY: 149.95.

Wide shot: Grosjan folding clothes

Medium shot: Grosjan puts his clothes into the wardrobe

GROSJAN: What I earn is... I only work part-time. And I earn about... Maybe 500

CENTRE SCREEN

BILAL: These are Diesel jeans. 110 euros.

Close-up: Bilal looks at himself

BILAL: 220 euros

Bilal looks in the mirror

BILAL: I spent 360 euro

MOUSSAD: My monthly wage is about 300 euros. So I just spend it all on shoes, jeans, tops...

From behind: Grosjan, bare-chested, fumbling with his boxer briefs and adjusting his waistline

RIGHT SCREEN

Benny looks back to see how his butt looks in the jeans

BENNY: I've got on an Armani T-shirt.

Grosjan puts on a pair of jeans

GROSJAN: These jeans are Levi's. These are 110 euros.

From behind: Grosjan folds his pants and turns around

GROSJAN: I haven't had this suit long. I got it the other day. It cost a pretty penny. I think more or less altogether, this and those shoes, must come to... maybe two, four, 800 euros. I spent about 1,800 guilders on this suit.

LEFT SCREEN

CENTRE SCREEN

RIGHT SCREEN

LEFT SCREEN

euros a month. Outside of school. And I also get money from my mother. And my father.

Wide shot: Grosjan from behind in white boxer briefs, he slowly puts on a T-shirt, checks his hair

Grosjan walks towards the wardrobe and takes a pair of pants. Pan from a close-up of Grosjan to Grosjan in the mirror, to Grosjan in front of the bed as he puts on a pair of jeans

Close-up: his hands covered with gold jewelry, buttoning up the jeans

CENTRE SCREEN

Grosjan lies on the bed and fiddles with his clothes, picking them up, touching them

GROSJAN: I come from a Muslim family and in our culture it's like: It's better to spend 5 euros on a T-shirt instead of 10 euros. With the other 5 euros you can help a poor family. When I show up with a 120 euro T-shirt I have to lie: Mama, it wasn't 120, it was 50 euros. I can't say the full price. My parents will make trouble.

RIGHT SCREEN

Shot of the wardrobe door; Bilal slowly comes into view

Bilal, a teenager with a grown man's face, very short black hair, the beginnings of a beard, takes of his pants.

BILAL: Prada is my favorite brand. I've got shoes from them at home. It's a very well-known brand in Italy. I like Versace too. That's a... clothes-maker for pants, and everything. I like them too. Armani is from Italy as well. I've got two of their pants at home.
They're all beautiful brands. But I think Prada is the most beautiful. I just bought some of

LEFT SCREEN	CENTRE SCREEN	RIGHT SCREEN

CENTRE SCREEN

Bilal smoothes his clothes, tucks his cuffs into his shoes

BILAL: At home I'm my father's pet. So he buys whatever I want. Even if it's expensive. Yeah, I have a nice father.

RIGHT SCREEN

their shoes. Cost 220 euros. That's why I love the brand so much.

Bilal checks his hair and clothes in the mirror

BILAL: Because I always do what he says. Because I do my best at school. He likes that. That's why he spoils me... With clothes.

LEFT SCREEN

Pan ending with Bilal sitting on the edge of the bed

BILAL: I want them to see me as a normal guy not someone who acts cool with his clothes. I don't want them thinking I show off with my clothes. I'm a normal guy.*

CENTRE SCREEN

Close-up: Bilal buttons up his shirt

RIGHT SCREEN

Bilal looking into the mirror, leaning back and forth, laughing

CENTRE SCREEN

Close-up: Bilal on the bed

BILAL: If I'm on the street, they look at me as if to say: Another Moroccan... I ignore it. I just walk on.

LEFT SCREEN

Yamahal, short black hair, muscular upper body, looks in the mirror, rubbing his shoulder, his upper arm and his neck

YAMAHAL: I work on my arms, my chest, my shoulders. I've been working out almost two

RIGHT SCREEN

Cuma, his hair gelled into spikes, sits on the edge of the bed folding a pair of pants

CUMA: I always want respect. I show respect for them so I want them to treat me with respect.**

Close-up: Yamahal from behind taking his T-shirt off.

CENTRE SCREEN

Yamahal's reflection in the mirror as he straightens his shirt

---

*See pages 48/49
**See page 44

LEFT SCREEN   CENTRE SCREEN   RIGHT SCREEN

years. Two years ago
I was really skinny.
I didn't dare go out in a
T-shirt.* They would have
laughed. But fortunately
it's very different now.
I don't mind taking
off my T-shirt.

180 degree pan around
Yamahal, who is putting on
a tight black T-shirt

YAMAHAL: I think clothes
come first. You have to
look good. For yourself,
so people can see you look
good. That's important.
Then they respect you
more. And you're cooler,
of course.** You buy
things other people can't
afford.

Moussad holds a pair of
pants up

Cuma's reflection
in the mirror

MOUSSAD: These are Replay
jeans. 110 euros.

CUMA: Iceberg jeans. 160
euros.

Close-up: Yamahal buttons
up his pants. He looks at
himself in the mirror

Cuma checks how his pants
fit in back

Yamahal pulls his
sleeves up a bit

Yamahal pulls a T-shirt
over his head

CUMA: Dolce & Gabbana. 140
euros.

YAMAHAL: Diesel.

Yamahal puts on a watch

YAMAHAL: I picked up this
Versace T-shirt. 110
euros.

YAMAHAL: I bought this
Diesel watch. Almost 100
euros.

Yamahal straightens his
hair while looking into
the mirror

Close-up: jeans being
pulled up

MOUSSAD: 40 euros.

<table>
<tr><td>LEFT SCREEN</td><td>CENTRE SCREEN</td><td>RIGHT SCREEN</td></tr>
</table>

LEFT SCREEN

Close-up: sneakers are put on

MOUSSAD: These are Pumas. This cost 70 euros.

Cuma puts on a beige shirt, 180 degree pan around him as he slowly buttons his shirt

CENTRE SCREEN

Cuma's reflection in the mirror. Shot from over his shoulder, he touches his face, turns his head in different directions to check it from all angles

CUMA: When I change my clothes, when I do my hair, when I see a mirror when I get somewhere, I want to look in the mirror...* To see if I look good, if my hair's OK, if my clothes are right. That they haven't got crumpled... Yeah...

Close-up: Cuma's face

CUMA: I know so many Dutch people in my class, they look like shit. They always stare at me. Hey, that guy looks good. Where's he get the money? Zoom out to Cuma sitting on the bed. But I'm the same as them. Just a student with a student grant. I only work part-time. I live at home. Our incomes are about the same... Look at me. Look at them. Pause. Most Dutch

RIGHT SCREEN

Cuma is sitting on the edge of the bed

CUMA: Most Dutch people have no style. They're too stingy.

*See pages 12/13

LEFT SCREEN | CENTRE SCREEN | RIGHT SCREEN

CENTRE SCREEN

parents say: Want to stay home after 18? Then pay rent. Otherwise you can go.

RIGHT SCREEN

Cuma on the bed fiddling with some keys

LEFT SCREEN

Cuma puts on a black shirt, careful of his hairdo

CENTRE SCREEN

Yamahal on the bed as he folds up his clothes

RIGHT SCREEN

CUMA: They're cold to their kids.

CENTRE SCREEN

YAMAHAL: It all started when I was 15. I started with a newspaper round. I remember getting my first pay. I bought Nikes right away. They were 200 guilders... That was my first pay, so I had to wait a whole month, working again to buy pants. They were Chipies. They were about the same, 200 or 300 guilders. So you worked all month for things... It's still the same, but fortunately I earn more now. I can combine it with paying the rent.

LEFT SCREEN

Pan over Yamahal's body as he puts on a black shirt

Yamahal on the bed folding a pair of jeans

RIGHT SCREEN

Close-up: Yamahal on the bed as he folds up his clothes

YAMAHAL: Now it's my wife who washes and irons my clothes. First it was my mother. It drove her crazy. I always had something new. This had to be washed like that, and that had to be washed like this. It's tough in a family with

LEFT SCREEN	CENTRE SCREEN	RIGHT SCREEN
	Close-up: shoes being taken off	six kids and one girl. Six boys and one girl.
	CUMA: In our culture it's like that. Cut to Cuma on the bed arranging his shoes. A woman has to do everything at home. Not everything. Well a man is supposed to help, but mostly the woman does it all. Cleaning and that... But when they have kids, they stay home. That's part of it. If they stay home, they have to wash and clean. He gets up and starts pulling his pants down. And the man has to work and bring home the money. He sits down and removes them completely. A Dutch woman? Not for me... I like Turkish girls, because I'm a Turk.	
Mutahir scans through the clothes in the wardrobe, then he arranges his boxers		Moussad looks at his boxers
MUTAHIR: My boxer shorts are called Dolce Gabbana. They cost 50 euros.		MOUSSAD: Nike. About 40 euros.
	Close-up: hands putting a belt through the belt loops	Pan around Cuma, who buttons up a beige shirt
Close-up: shoe being put on, hands straightening laces, pants	YAMAHAL: Armani, Evisu.	CUMA: I'm wearing Energy. 130 euros.

Each day, I change my outfit at least three times. It takes about three hours a day.

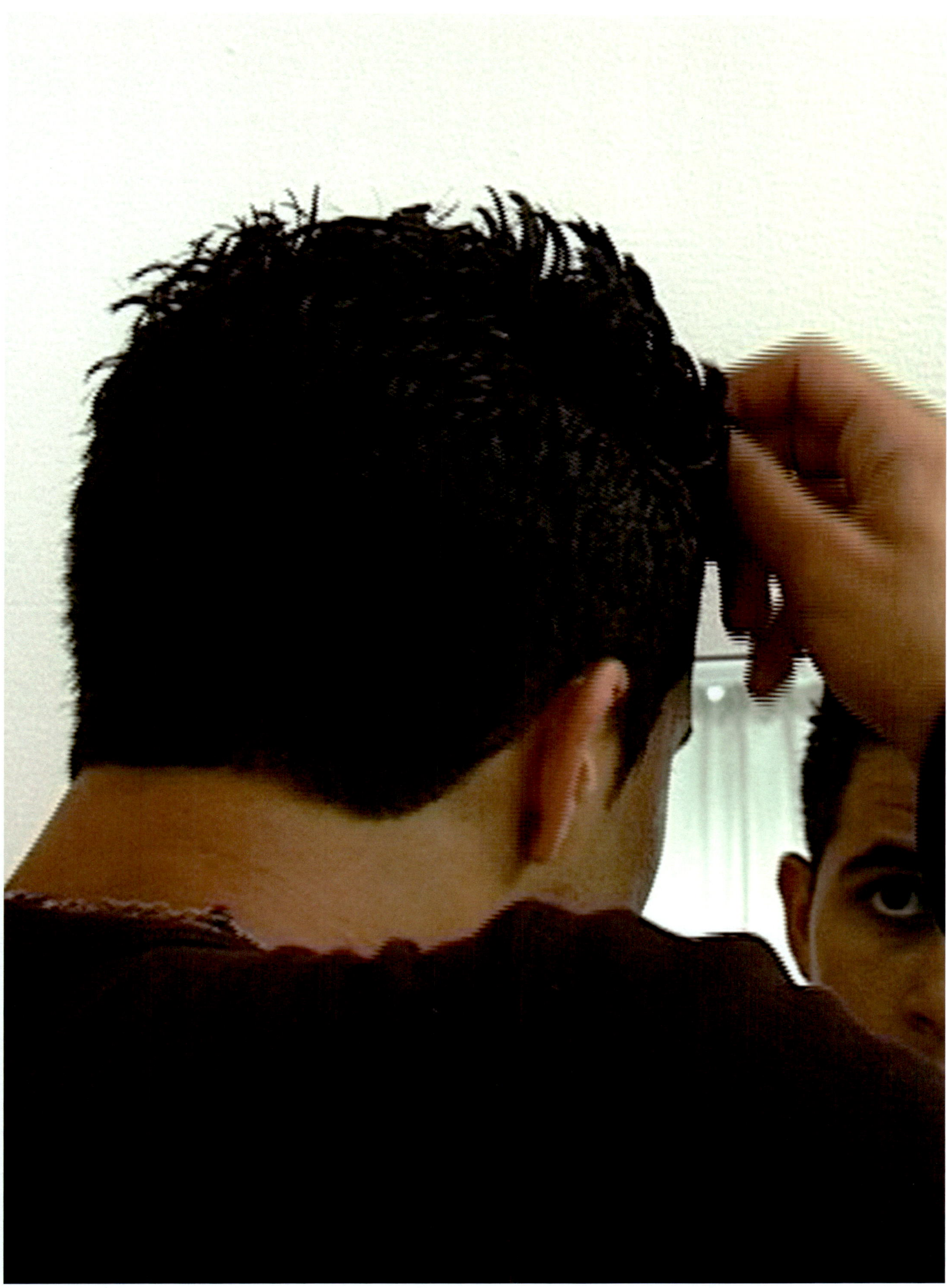

Read page 63

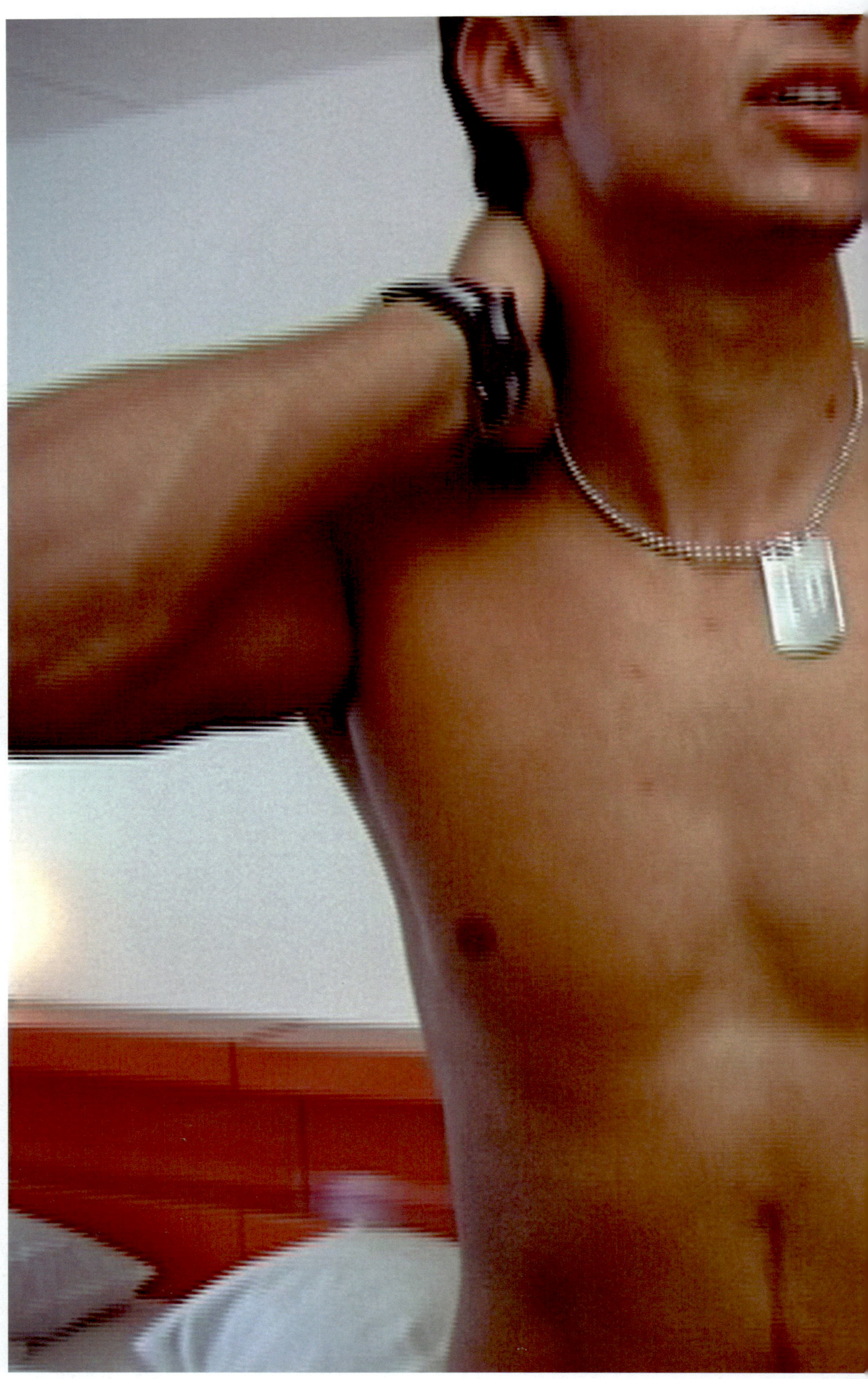

Read page 55

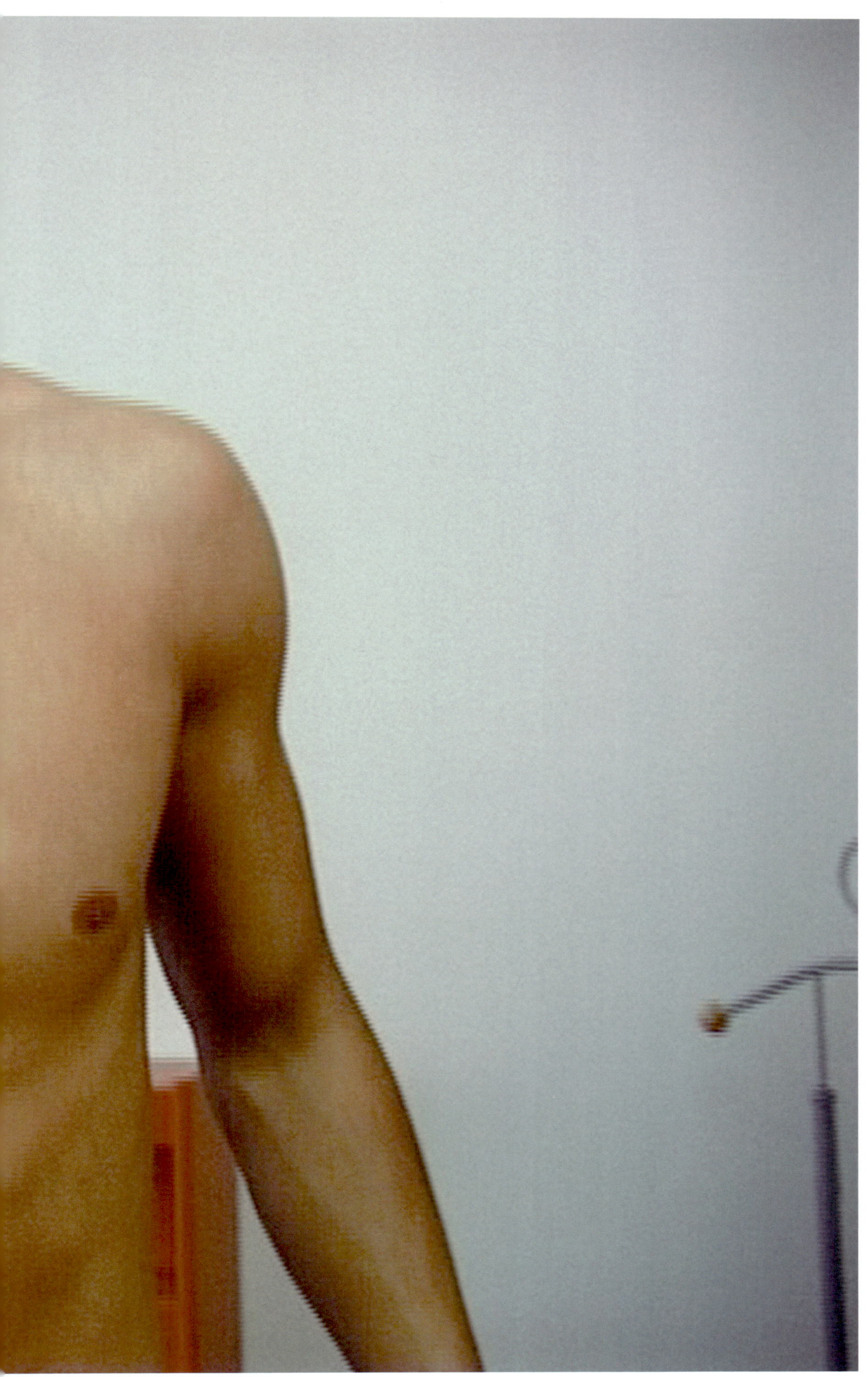

I just wanted to belong. I worked hard for that coat. But it is good quality. It'll last.

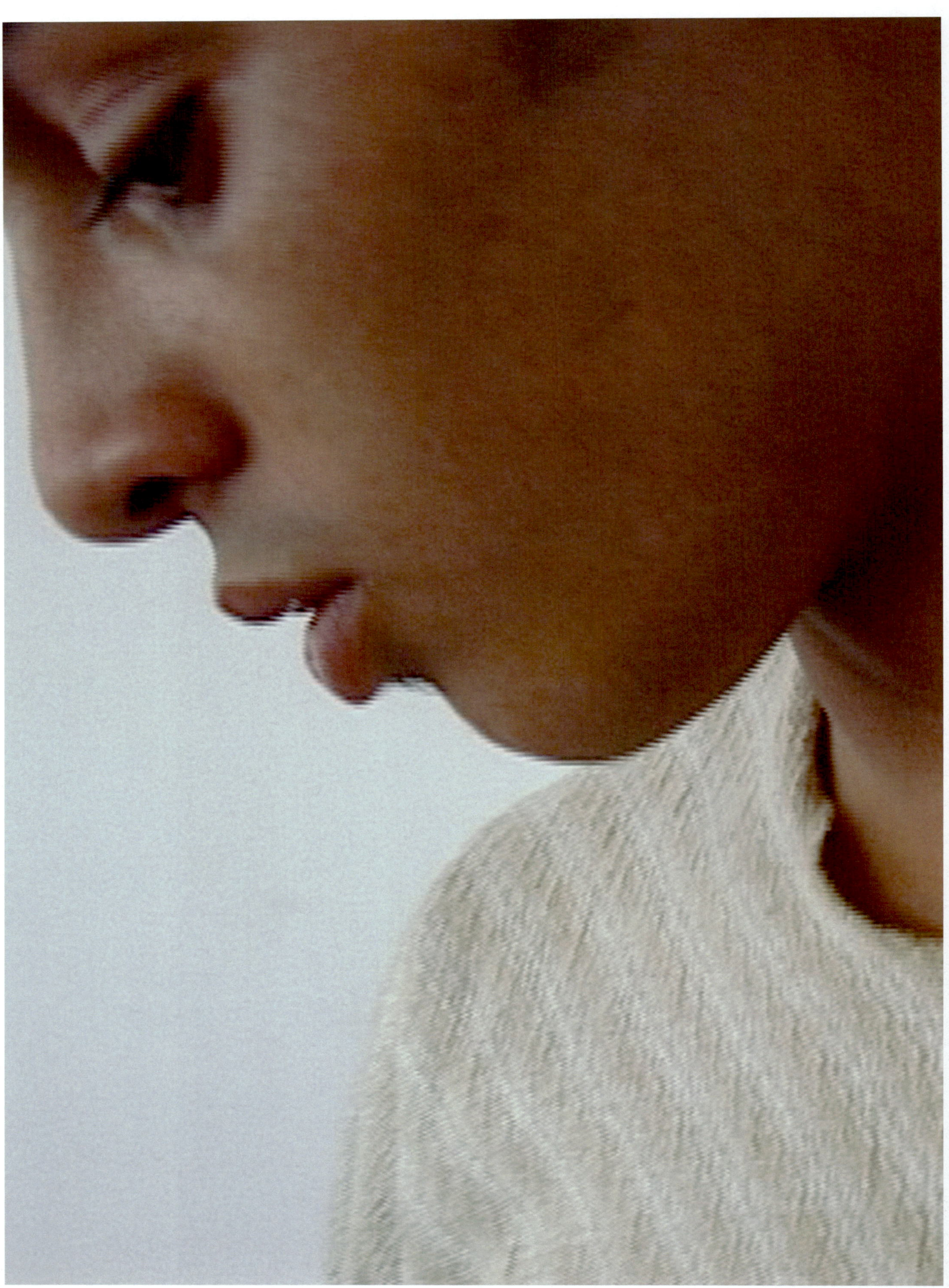

Read page 51

| LEFT SCREEN | CENTRE SCREEN | RIGHT SCREEN |

GROSJAN: Pradas. 220 euros.

Mutahir folds up clothes on the bed. He picks up a shirt on a hanger, looks at it, straightens it

He puts clothes into the wardrobe

Mutahir unbuttons his shirt, walks towards the bed and leafs through his clothes looking for another shirt

Pan over the shoes and pants Cuma is wearing

CUMA: I'm wearing Moschino. 200 euros. Prada. 250 euros.

Close-up: feet in low socks, hands arranging the hair on his legs. Pan up and towards the mirror Mutahir looks at his reflection

MUTAHIR: I always put on something different if I'm going somewhere. If I visit someone, I get changed. If I go to the playground or the square, I get changed. If I go out, I get changed. Each day, I change my outfit at least three times. It takes about three hours a day.* If you add it all up, changing my clothes. He goes closer to the mirror, runs his fingers over his face and through his hair. I don't always have the same hairstyle. Sometimes my hair's like this and sometimes it's flat. He arranges his gelled spikes of hair. And if I don't feel like doing my hair, if there's nothing important on then I just wash it and go out like that... But of course I don't stay out long...

*See page 59

<table>
<tr><td>LEFT SCREEN</td><td>CENTRE SCREEN</td><td>RIGHT SCREEN</td></tr>
</table>

CENTRE SCREEN

Mutahir, bare-chested,
sits back on the bed

MUTAHIR: I love looking
in the mirror... And I
love... I always want to
make sure that I look
very good. So that people
won't talk about me,
saying: He doesn't bother.
His colours clash or his
clothes don't go together.
Or he's ugly. I don't
want to ever hear things
like that... And well...
because I've never heard
it yet I'm very self-
confident. I have faith in
myself. Even if I put on a
shirt worth 1 or 2 euros,
it looks good on me.
That doesn't bother me.

Close-up: Mutahir's face
in profile

MUTAHIR: Externals come
first for me. And what's on
the inside comes second...
Well...

LEFT SCREEN

He puts on a white shirt

RIGHT SCREEN

I don't want other people
talking about me saying
I've got a bad haircut.

Pan towards Cuma's face

CUMA: I'm still young.
I'll only live once. I get
one youth, so I make sure
I spend it right.

Pan from Cuma's hands,
which are playing with the
string of a bag, towards
his face

CUMA: Why not look good?
When will you get another
chance? You only live
once, as I just said.

| LEFT SCREEN | CENTRE SCREEN | RIGHT SCREEN |

Cuma closes the wardrobe, walks towards the bed, sits down, gets up again, cleans up his clothes, walks around, sits down again

Mutahir sits on the bed

MUTAHIR: If I, for example, go out and if I'm looking really bad, people won't come up to talk to me to find out what I'm really like on the inside. I just try to look good. If I look good, they find out what I'm like on the inside, they get to know me. Well, that's what it's like for me.

Cuma's reflection in the mirror, he looks at himself

CUMA: It's nice if your girlfriend looks good and you look good for her. It's nice to look good together, isn't it? Birds of a feather flock together. You can't get along, if one looks good and the other one doesn't.

Close-up: Mutahir looks at himself in the mirror, plucks at his T-shirt, straightens his pants, turns around and looks at his butt

Mutahir lingers on the bed

MUTAHIR: Once I'm married, I'll stop. It won't matter to me whether I look good or bad. At least, I'll always try to look good... I'll have someone who will stay with me. So I won't have to go out chasing girls and I won't need compliments from girls... It will be all over for me.

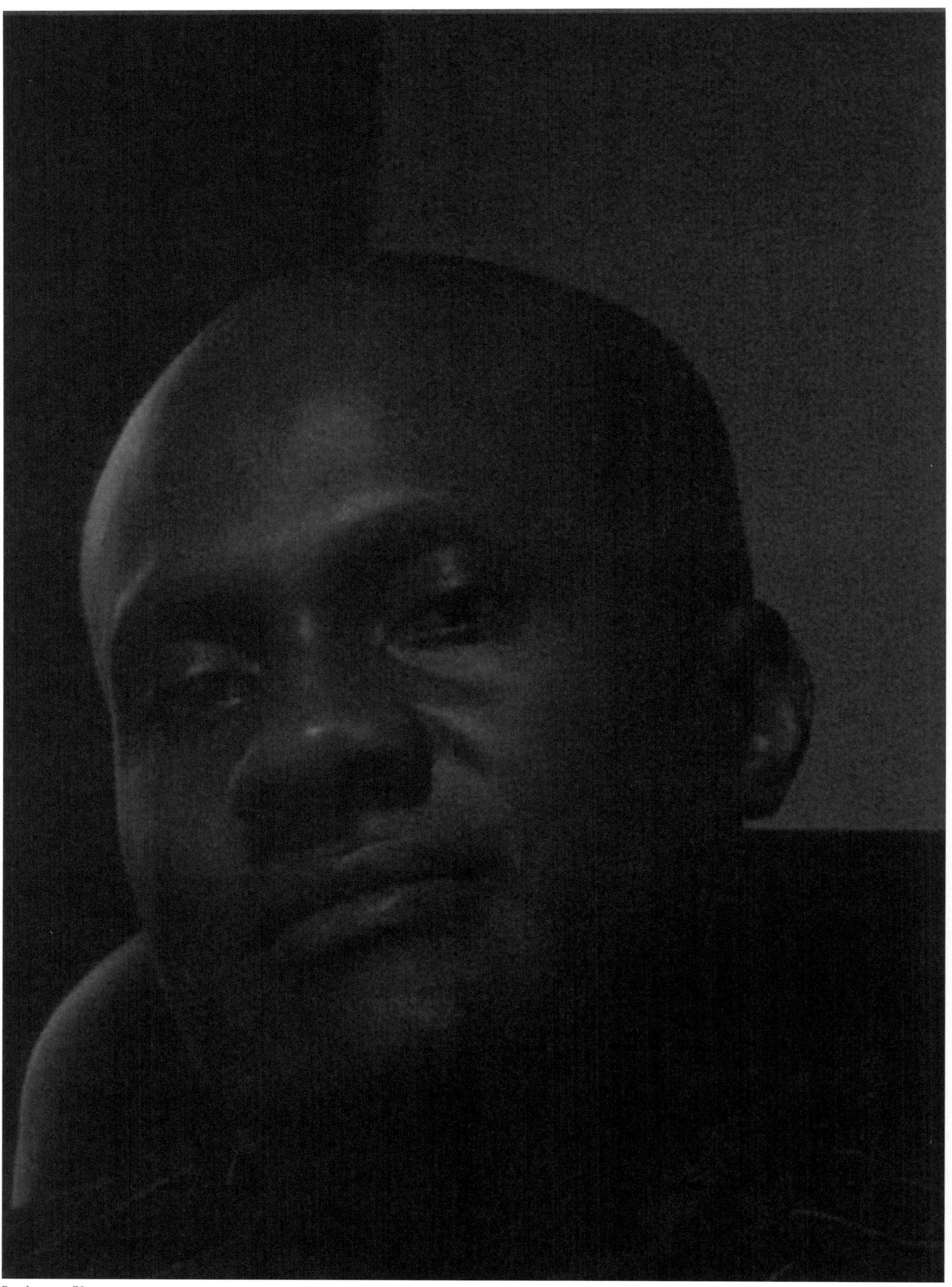

YOUR BLOOD IS AS RED
AS MINE

Video projection, 15:56
min, dvd, subtitled,
2004

With: Chicco, Ivan, Jean
Paul, Ambrose, Anthony,
Ibrahim, Nelson, Layla,
Raymon

With the assistance of:
Martin Hansen

Camera: Julika Rudelius
Editing: Martin Hansen
Subtitles: Erik Pezarro

Thanks to:
Helle Lyshøj, Bert
Oosterveld, Marieken
Verheyen, Thomas van
der Linde, Theresa Ley,
Mark Bain, Marty Lamers
and Frederique Bergholz

Funded by:
Centrum Beeldende Kunst
Zuidoost and Stedelijk
Museum Bureau Amsterdam

YOUR BLOOD IS AS RED AS MINE

VIDEO PROJECTION
15:56 MIN
DVD
SUBTITLED
2004

A silver BMW, racing wheels, tinted windows, in front of a white wall. Chicco is listening to loud rap music, moving his head to the rhythm, holding the steering wheel with one outstretched hand. Julika approaches the car from behind and gets in. A few moments later, the car slowly rolls out of view. The sound gets reduced to the bass of the car stereo, which makes the plastic and metal parts of the car rattle.

Ivan and Julika in a room that resembles a cafeteria. Julika sits on the counter, leaning against a wall with white kitchen tiles

IVAN: We're used to that in Surinam. In Surinam we have different races. Discrimination is something we learnt here in Holland.
JULIKA: What do you mean?
IVAN: That people judge you on the colour of your skin.

Julika gets off the counter and sits opposite from Ivan at the table. The wall behind Ivan is covered with light-brown wooden panels. The camera films from over Julika's shoulder, facing Ivan

JULIKA: What's it like being black?
IVAN: What's it like? It's hard to explain because I don't feel black.
JULIKA: Not at all?
IVAN: No, I just feel like a human being.
JULIKA: But... when I come here to the Bijlmer, I suddenly feel very white.
IVAN: I can imagine. If I go to a white suburb like Wassenaar... I do feel black then.
JULIKA: Should one say 'black' or 'coloured'?
IVAN: I don't really care.
JULIKA: If I see couples, the women are generally lighter than the men. Why is that?
IVAN: Men, black men, are just attracted to lighter-skinned women.
JULIKA: But why?
IVAN: Maybe, if you think of reproduction, if two very black people like that have kids together, you'll definitely get one like that. But, I think, if one's lighter and the other one's darker... then you get something in between, I think.
JULIKA: And that's more beautiful?
IVAN: Sure. Isn't it? Yeah, in a way that's what black people say. Take Michael

                    Jackson. He's disgraced the black race by doing what he's done.
JULIKA: He looks terrible too.
IVAN: Yeah, like a ghost.

The table filmed from above. You see the arms of Ivan on the table. Julika's chin is
resting in her hand. After a while, she moves a hand close to Ivan's arms*

Jean Paul stands on a bed in a really small room. He is moving the red curtains which
bathe the whole room in red light. Loud reggae music is playing.

JULIKA: Could you open it all the way? Otherwise it's so red.

Julika comes in and bends over to take her boots off

JEAN PAUL: Can we use the parlour? Jean Paul steps off the bed and walks out of the
                room. Is the parlour OK?

Jean Paul and Julika in a living room. There is a dark leather couch, a dining table
with matching oak chairs and green velvet cushions, a fake wooden floor. The room is
bathed in bright daylight. They sit at the table. Julika is holding a Polaroid. We hear
the same reggae song in the background, but the volume is lower

JULIKA: You're not supposed to look at the pose...Where would you like to be seen in
                this room?
JEAN PAUL: I don't have a specific position.
JULIKA: But how would you like to see yourself?
JEAN PAUL: I just want to see myself in a very nice way... The white hand. Comfortable.

Ambrose sits in a living room on a white couch. There is a mahogany floor, designer lamps
turned on. The dark blue of evening shows through the curtains behind him

AMBROSE: So what do you want to talk about?
JULIKA: I don't know. I... Julika walks into the frame holding a glossy magazine. She
                sits on the matching armchair next to Ambrose. If you look at this... I just
                think that the pictures are quite overexposed.

*See pages 72/73

AMBROSE: Overexposed? What pictures?

Cut-away: close-up shots of a magazine page with photos of black celebrities

JULIKA: Here, look at this. If it looks so overexposed, it's just odd. Why do they do
            it? Do they want to be whiter, or something like this?
AMBROSE: Whiter? Where did you get that from? Look at this face, for example. If you
            made this a little darker you wouldn't see the whole features. Look at the
            eyes, look at the nose, look at everything. You make it a little darker, you
            lose half of it. This is a horrible picture.
JULIKA: That's true.

Cut-away: close-up of another magazine page. The celebrity is so black that we cannot
see his face against the dark background

AMBROSE: You only see a black spot on the head. You don't see a face. It's just about
            light, that's all. I mean, contrast. It's not about making people white...
            Absolutely not. That's the last thing we want to do... They would kill us if
            we did that. Definitely.

Close-up: Anthony sits in an office chair in front of a window. He is backlit and is
holding a baby. The sound of the murmuring baby mixes with the sound of a microwave in
the background

JULIKA: Could you now put on a suit?
ANTHONY: Put on a suit?
JULIKA: Yeah. I'll take the baby.

Anthony gets up, Julika's back comes into the frame, her hands grab the baby and put him
on her hip

Close-up: Anthony's face, which is so dark that only a faint blue outline of light
makes his head visible. We hear the technical sounds of a camera being operated

JULIKA: Don't move, OK?*

*See page 66

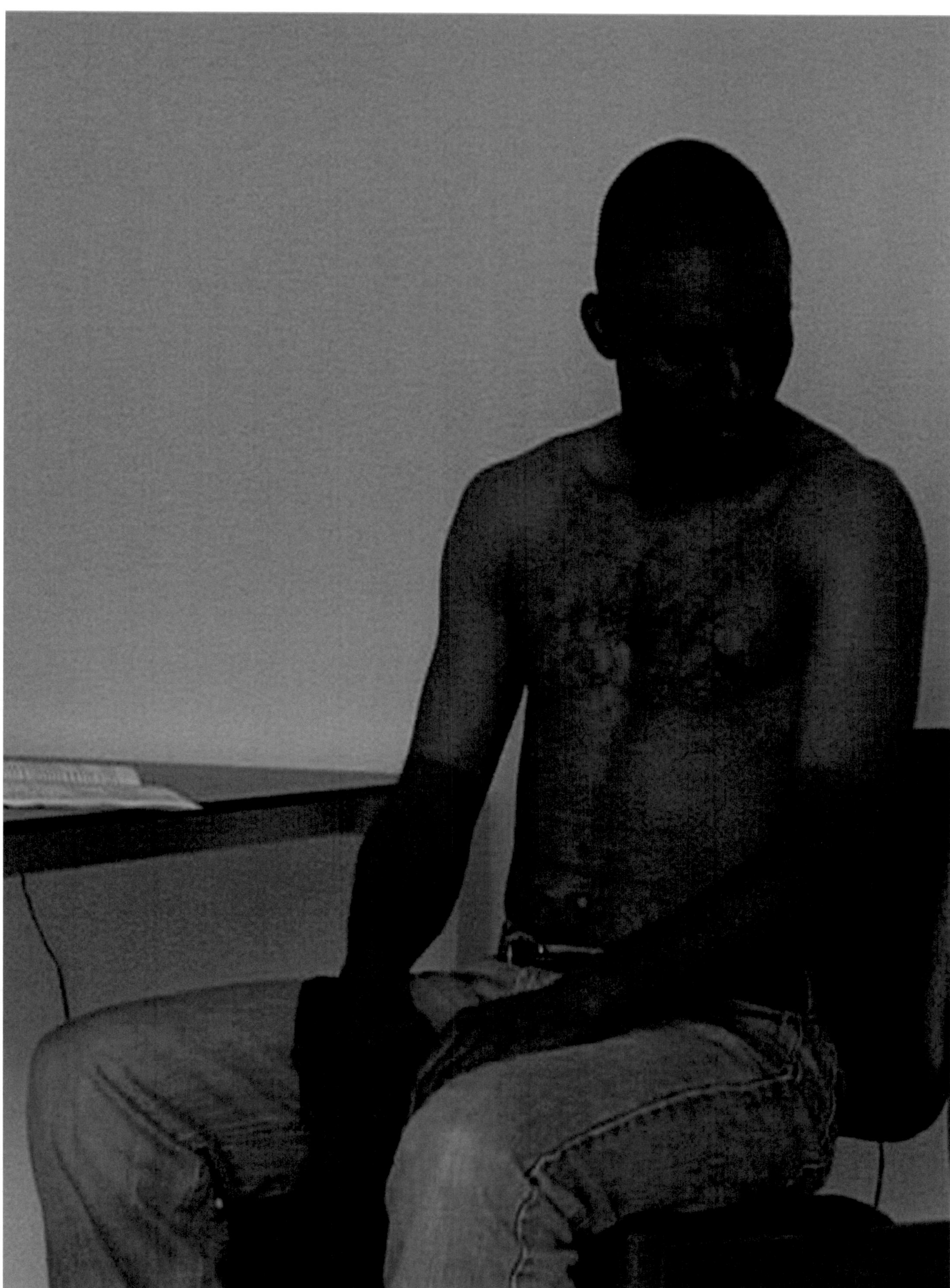

Read page 81

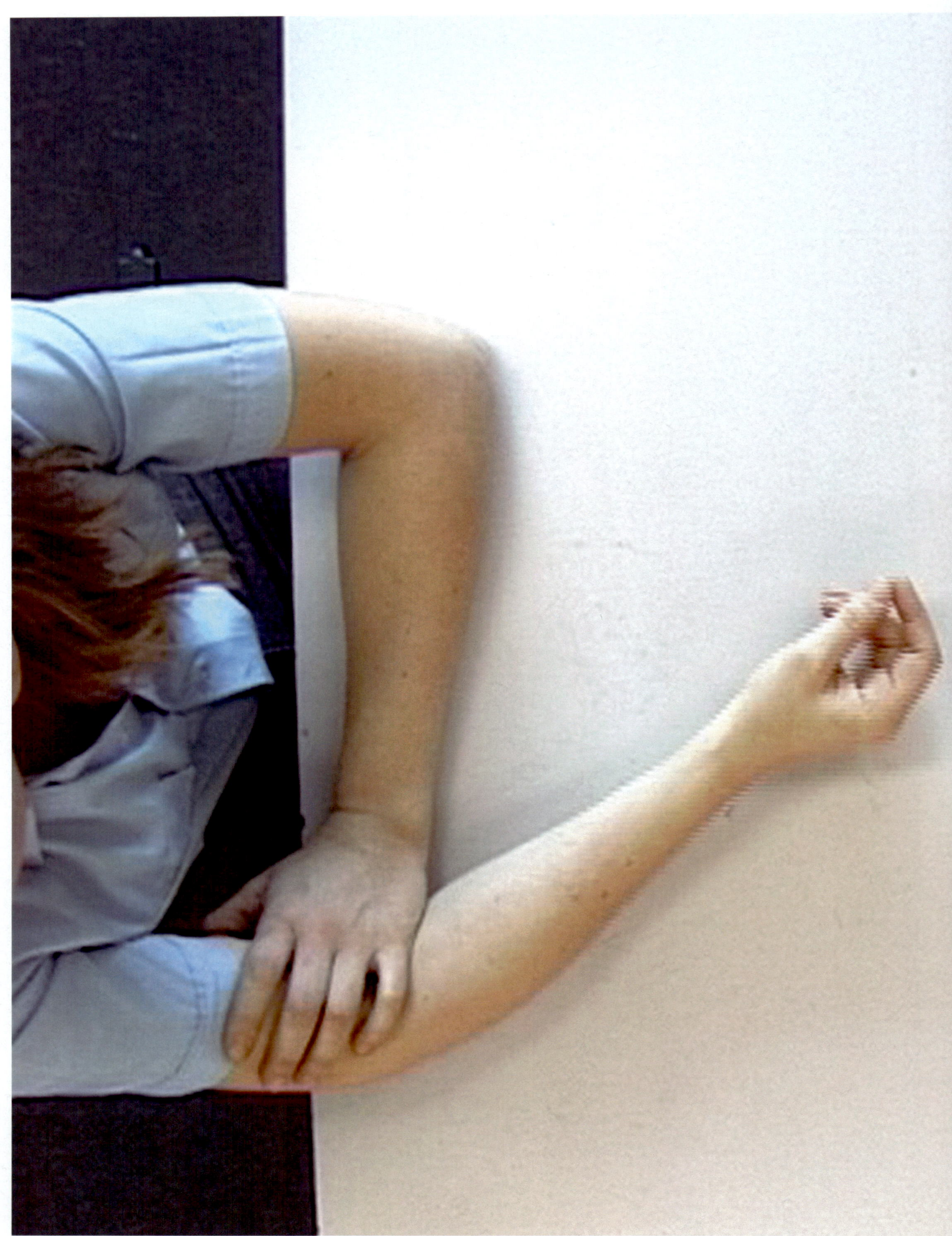

Read page 69

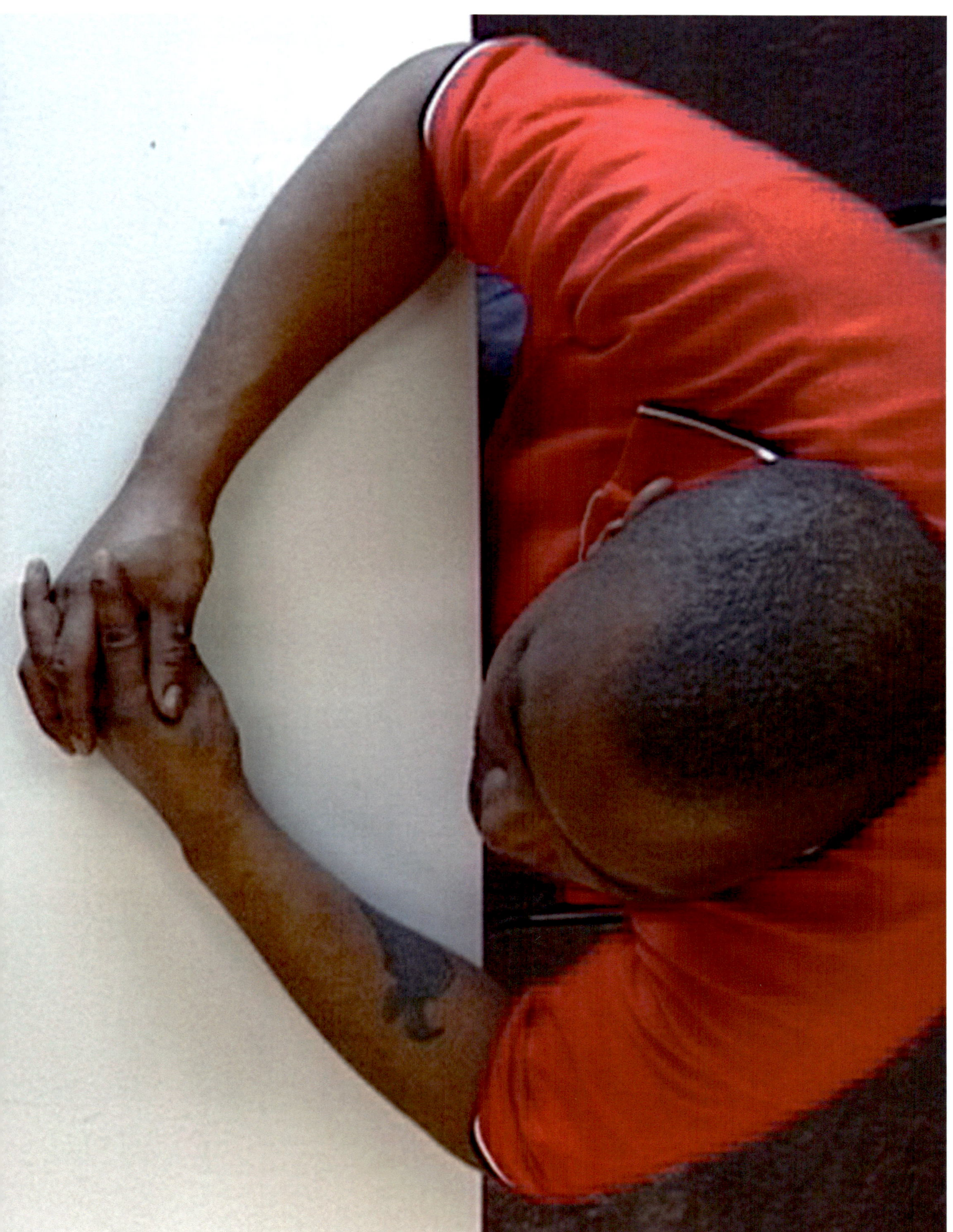

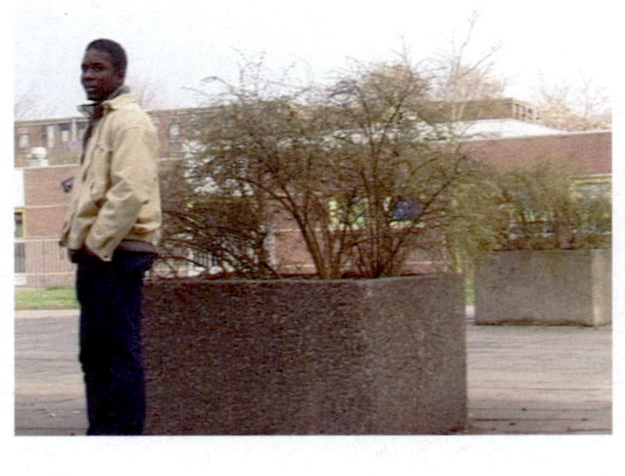 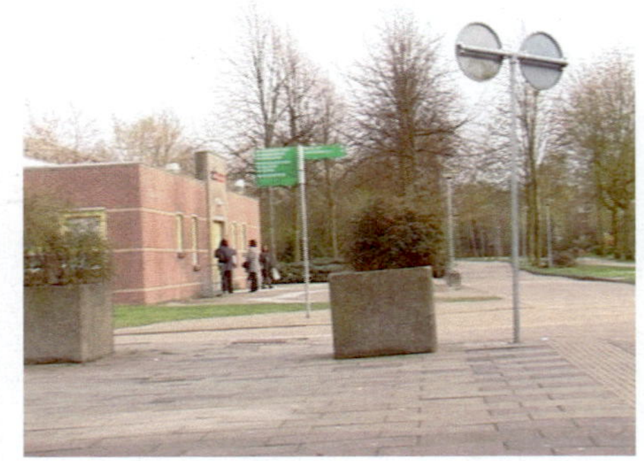 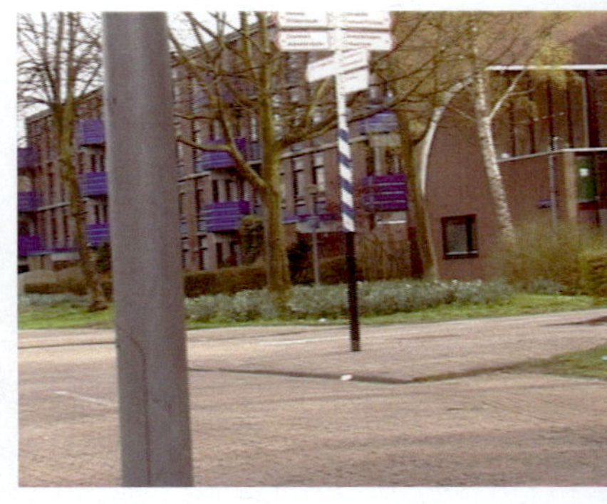
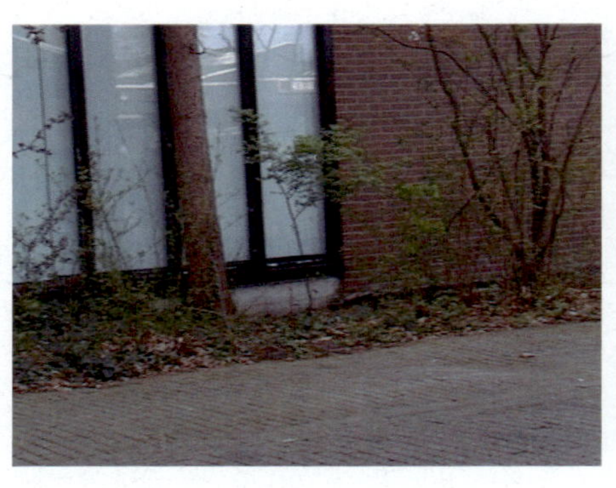 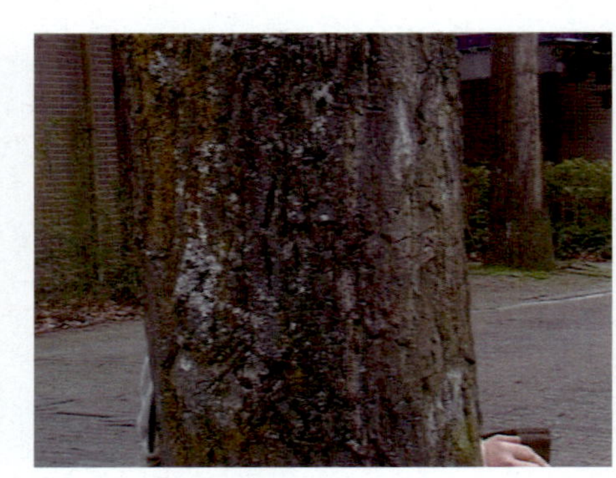 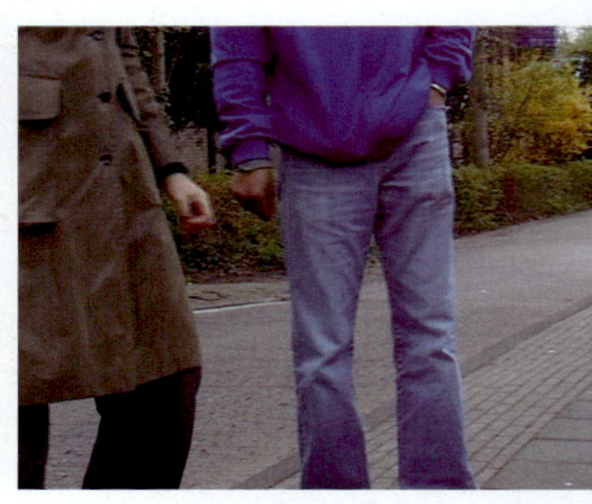
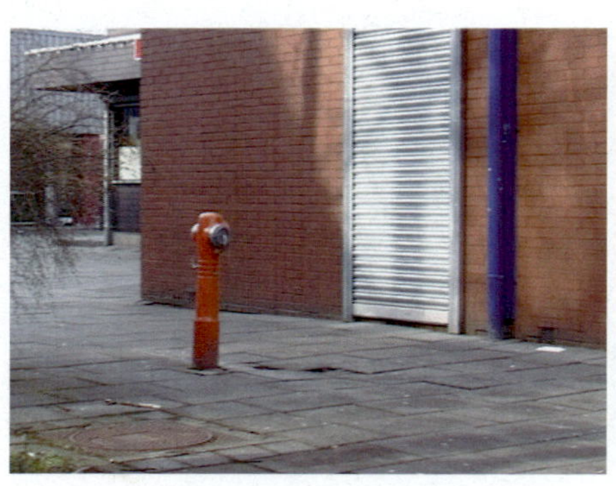 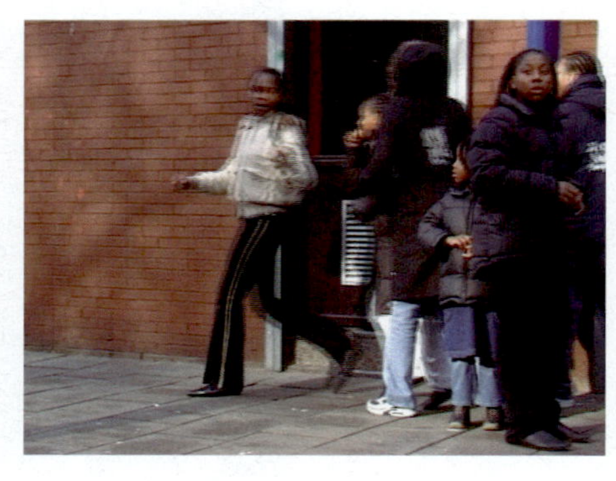 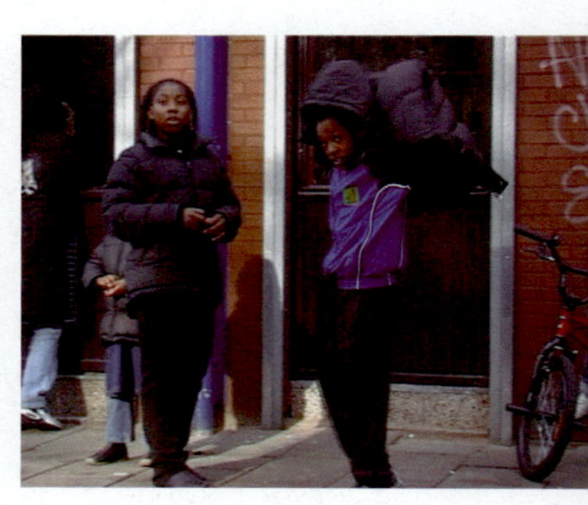
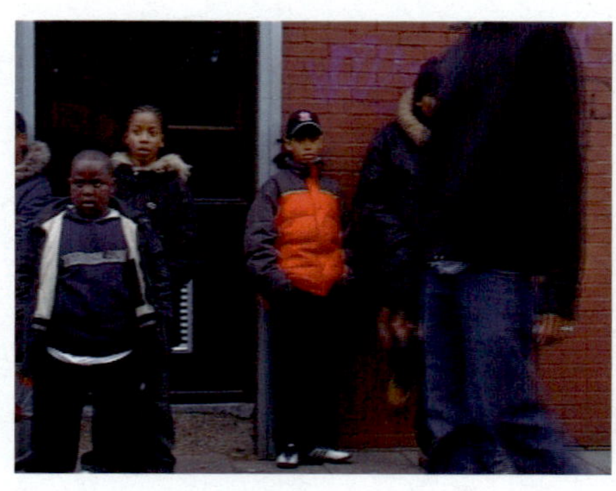 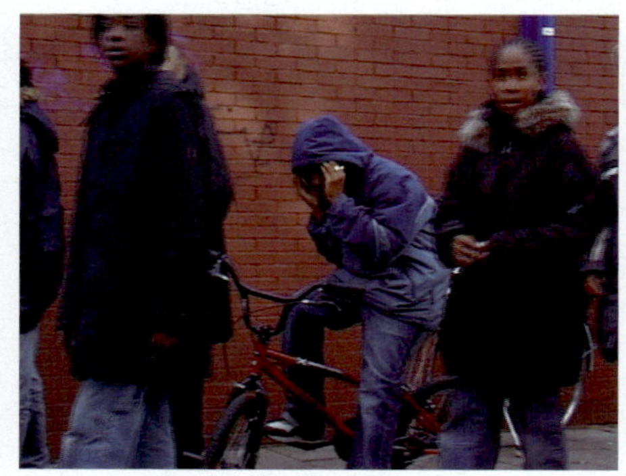 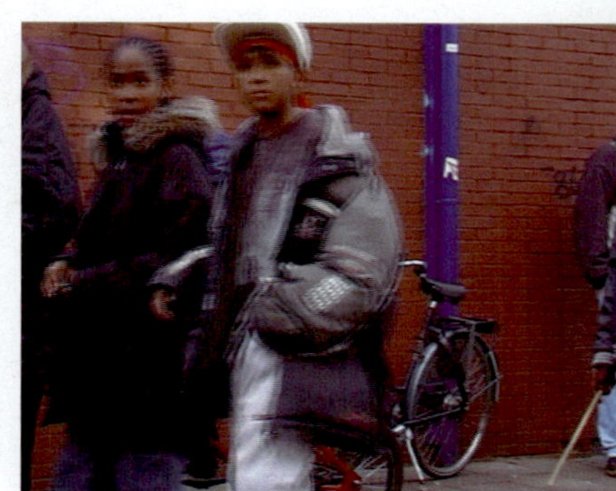

Read page 81

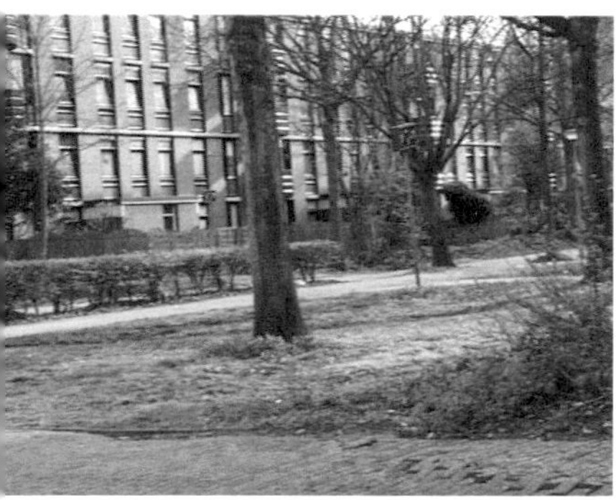
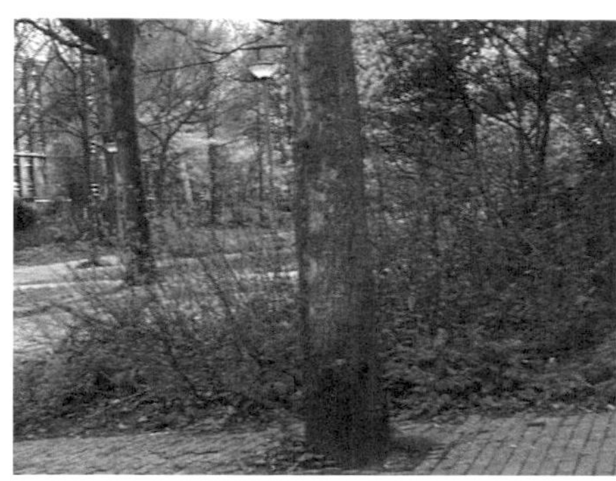
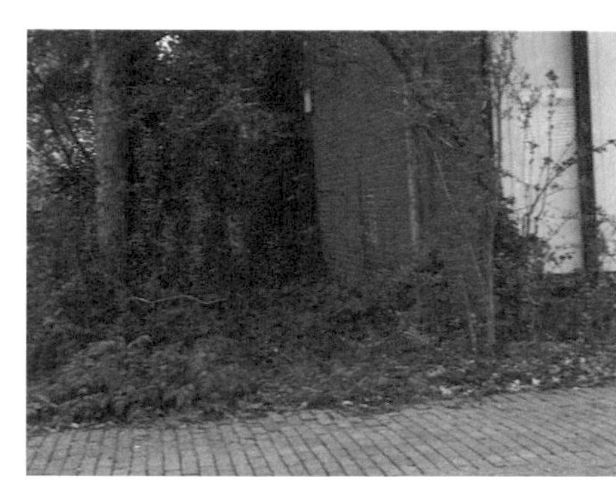
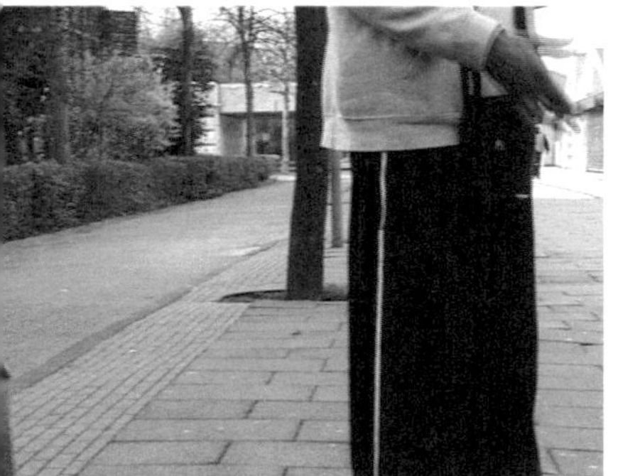
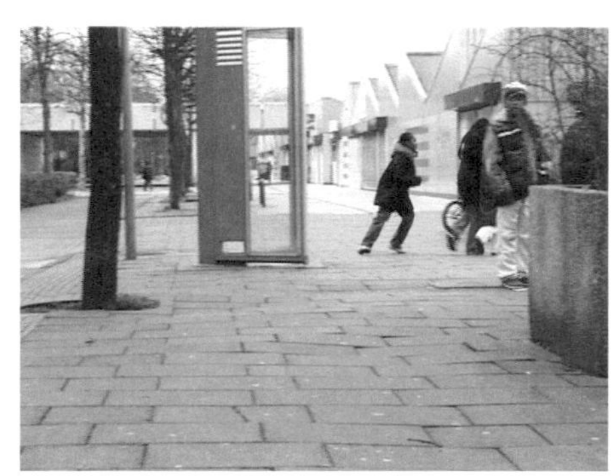
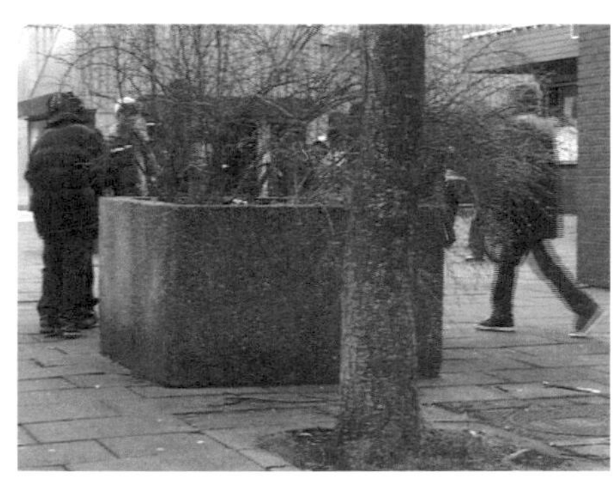
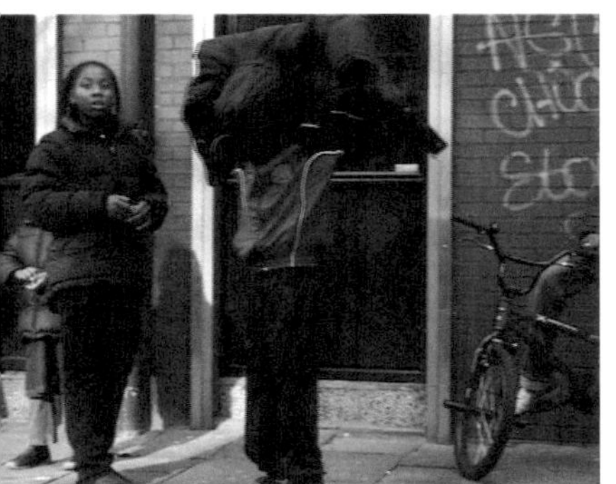
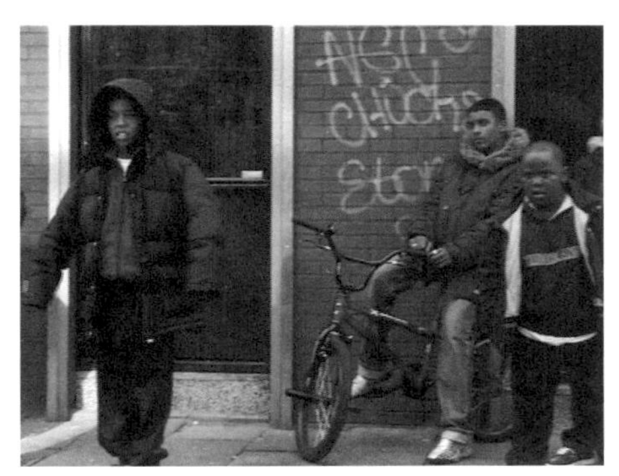
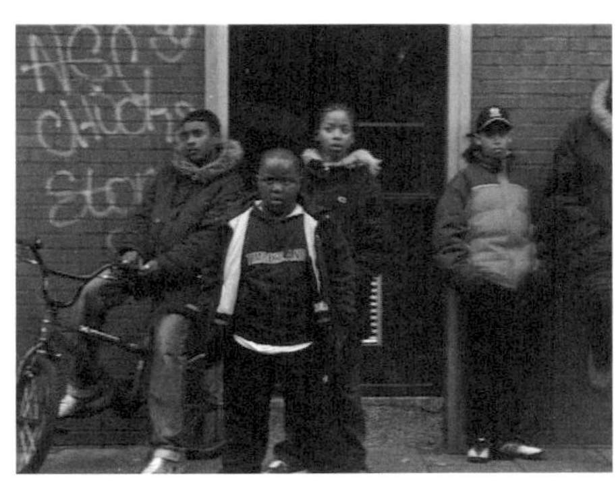
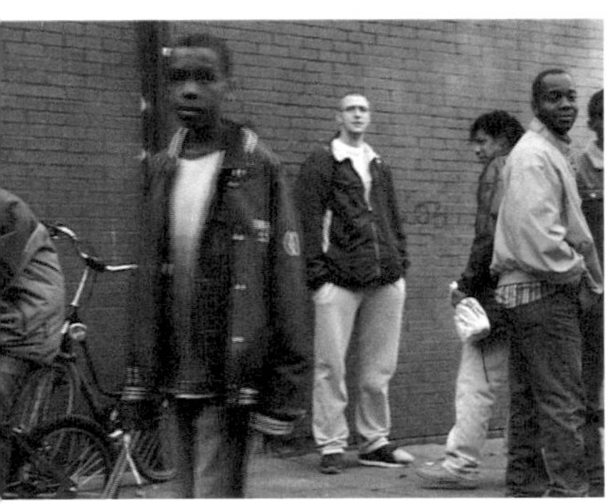
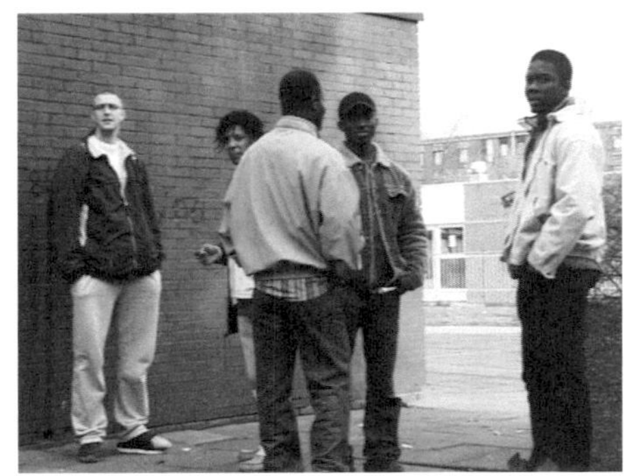

The flash goes off and Anthony's face is fully visible for a split second, then there is darkness again

Zoom out from Anthony, who holds a white piece of paper in front of his head

JULIKA: Oh, that's really blue. Zoom in so that you only see the white paper; the colour changes from blue to red to white. Do you still like modelling?
ANTHONY: It was fun, anyway. You meet a lot of people... But sometimes I discover I'm the only black there.
JULIKA: You're doing the what? The black bear?
ANTHONY: Sometimes I discover I'm the only black.

Frontal shot of Chicco and Julika in a moving car. Chicco is driving

JULIKA: What do you want?
CHICCO: Just Dubbel Friss.
JULIKA: Which flavour?
CHICCO: Whatever, doesn't matter.
JULIKA: Come on, Chicco... I don't know about that stuff. If you don't tell me...
CHICCO: It's peach and whatsit. Peach and... grape. I don't care.

The car stops and Julika gets out. She slams the door, which causes the frame to jump

JULIKA: They didn't have any larger bottles.
CHICCO: No, they're like that.

In front of a white background, we see a crowd of black, male heads from behind. We hear the sound of a priest talking in English and a woman translating into Dutch. The heads start nodding in agreement and hands sway above them

PRIEST: ...get beyond your enemies, hallelujah...

Clapping, more hands in the air

A hotel room, daylight. Ibrahim sits in a red armchair, next to him there is an oversized cross made from plywood. Julika walks into the frame with a light-meter. She measures light in front of Ibrahim and walks out of the frame again

Close-up: Ibrahim's face in dim, artificial light

JULIKA: You also want to find out about me?
IBRAHIM: Absolutely. I said, 'You are one of my own case studies too.' Julika laughs. She bends into the frame so that only the back of her head can be seen. You're here to study me, I'm here to study you. Part of the reason why I said, 'OK, let's talk.' Julika's head bends back. Ibrahim's head is visible but out of focus at first, then the auto-focus adjusts. This happens every time Julika's head comes into the frame. As you try to sound me out, I want to sound you out... Like I said, I'm using you as my model kind of person. I want to reach out... Why you? One, you're Caucasian... Two, you have the general mentality of the average white European... You believe a lot in reason... You want to relate to what you can feel and experience and see not just what you imagine... And...

Medium shot: Ibrahim seated in front of a stack of books, same light

IBRAHIM: Julika... Life is not only about living here. Tell me, what's the purpose of your life?
JULIKA: Make good work.
IBRAHIM: That's the purpose?
JULIKA: Yeah. Julika covers the frame. Make something... to make good art.
IBRAHIM: That's why you were born?
JULIKA: But I make... Sometimes I hope that I make art which other people will bring somewhere.
IBRAHIM: That's why? That's all? Why you were born?... So when you die, what happens?
JULIKA: Probably some people will still look at my pictures or my films.
IBRAHIM: And what happens to you?
JULIKA: I'm dead.
IBRAHIM: And what happens? Does it end there?
JULIKA: Yeah, I'm quite sure.
IBRAHIM: No life after death?

JULIKA: No, of course not.

IBRAHIM: Are you absolutely sure? What if when you die you discover there's life after
            death?

JULIKA: I will deal with it then.

IBRAHIM: Would you be in a position to deal with it then?

JULIKA: I think I've lived my life... when there is a Judgement or something like
            this... I think I've lived my life quite OK. Julika starts laughing, covers
            the frame. Until now. No, but I think, I try not to harm people and I try
            to...

IBRAHIM: Don't be silly.

JULIKA: Well, it's true!

IBRAHIM: It's such a serious matter that you don't just use some very... Ibrahim
            frowns, then laughs too. Julika laughs and bends down under the table. No,
            because I see people live life. And the sad thing about life is that this
            life is a fleeting life.

Nelson in a white room, with only one leaf of a houseplant hanging into the frame. He
stands with one hand resting on a mantelpiece, his right hand in his pocket. Daylight

JULIKA: Can you look in the camera? Nelson turns and flashes a quick, artificial smile,
            then a cell phone rings. That's your telephone, do you want to take it?

NELSON: Can I?

JULIKA: Yes, will you come back then?

Nelson walks out of the frame, comes back with his cell phone

NELSON: No, I'm still busy here.

JULIKA: We'll go in ten minutes.

NELSON: But you've finished the printing, right? I'll pay for it. You can give it to
            them. I'll give you the money tonight. So I'm making a... model in my house.

Nelson's landline rings.

NELSON: No, this is not what I want.

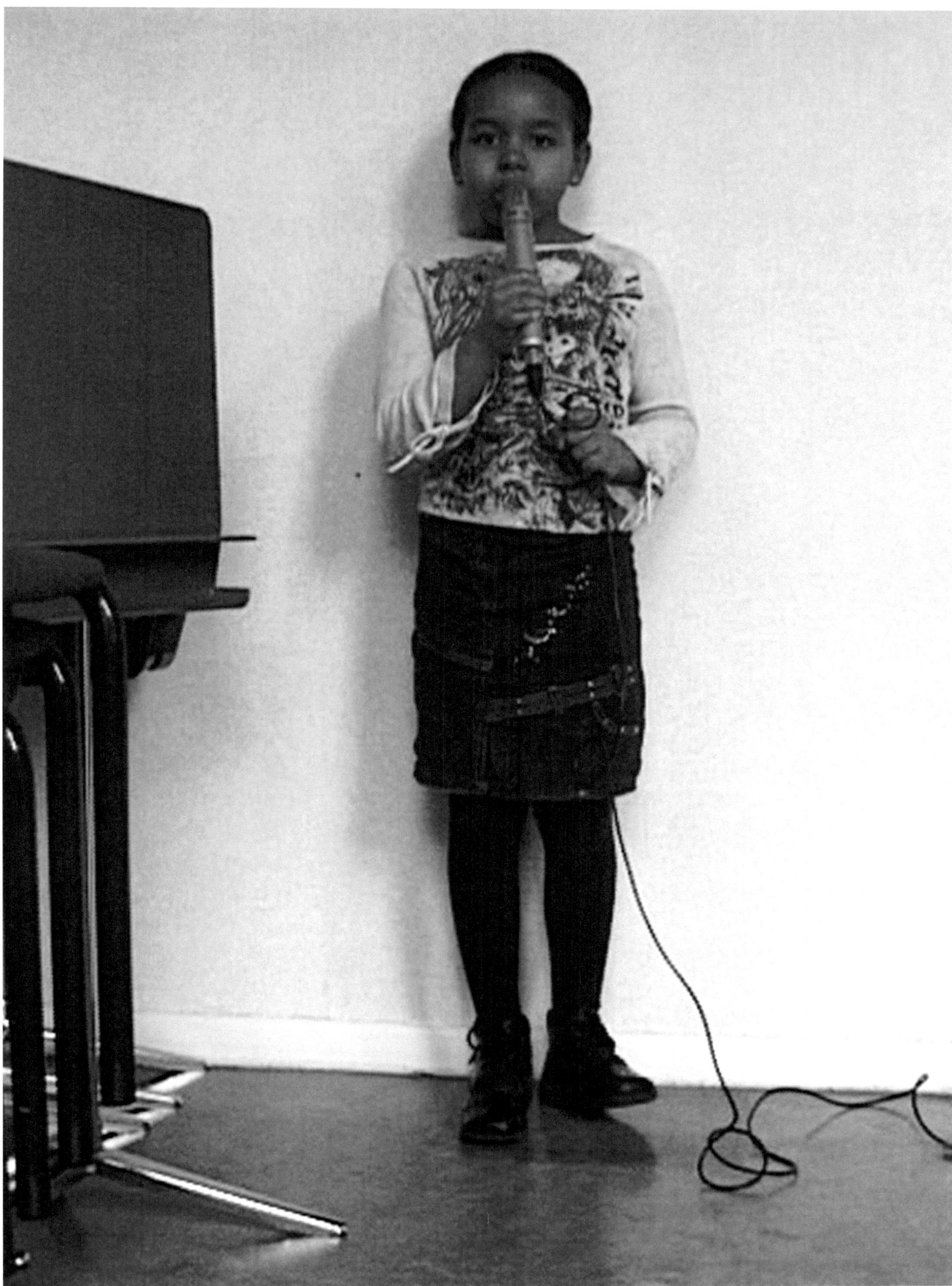

Read page 80

Julika brings this phone into the frame, too. Nelson talks into both phones. After a while, Julika comes into the frame and moves Nelson, who is still talking into both phones, back to the original position beside the mantelpiece

Nelson in a different suit, sitting in a chair in the same room, tying his shoelaces, humming to himself

Nelson poses in the chair, and the flash of the camera goes off

NELSON: What are you doing?

Julika comes into the frame. She laughs, grabs his hands and helps him out of the chair

JULIKA: That was with a blurry head. That's nice.
NELSON: Is it?

Close-up: Layla's head with a microphone. She is singing very skillfully: 'I Keep on Fallin'' from Alicia Keys*

JULIKA: Go on.

The camera moves out slowly until we see Layla from head to toe. She is standing in between a door and some chairs. Her shoulders just reach the door handle, revealing her young age**

Daylight. Raymond sits in a living room at a modern dining table with a cordless phone, a coffee cup and a newspaper on it. He is wearing a T-shirt and examines his bare arms and hands. The flash goes off

RAYMOND: I take it off?

He takes off his T-shirt and looks at himself. He is already black, but his head and his arms (up to where his shirtsleeves were) are distinctively darker. Julika walks into the frame and looks at him

JULIKA: It's really brown. Beautiful.

Julika starts cleaning up the table

JULIKA: Thanks a lot... Do you want to take a look at yourself?... How you look now?*
            They walk out of the frame. But don't scream.

Frontal shot of Chicco and Julika in an idling car. Loud R&B music is playing, and with every bass beat the camera shakes to the rhythm

Two cameras on a rotating tripod, filming medium shots at chest level. A city square during the day. The place slowly fills up with black kids of all ages. They are kicking a ball around and talking

OFF-SCREEN MALE VOICE: Denzil, what are you doing? The kids stop playing. Denzil, what are you doing there? The camera goes by a man who is shouting. We can only see his torso. Do you know who this is? Well shut up then. I don't take your camera and take it away? The kids start staring, both at the man and the camera. You come here and film children and take that away. Do their parents know? Now all the kids are staring. Soon their parents will come and ask, 'What were you filmed for?' 'I dunno.' You're a witch. Piss off. The kids start leaving the square. What are you doing here? Do you live here?** Who are these kids? Have you ever seen them before? What's one of these kids' names? Tell me the name of one of these kids. All kids and the speaker leave the square. You'll show them on TV hanging out on the corner they never hang out on. The next time the cameras go by, the square is empty.

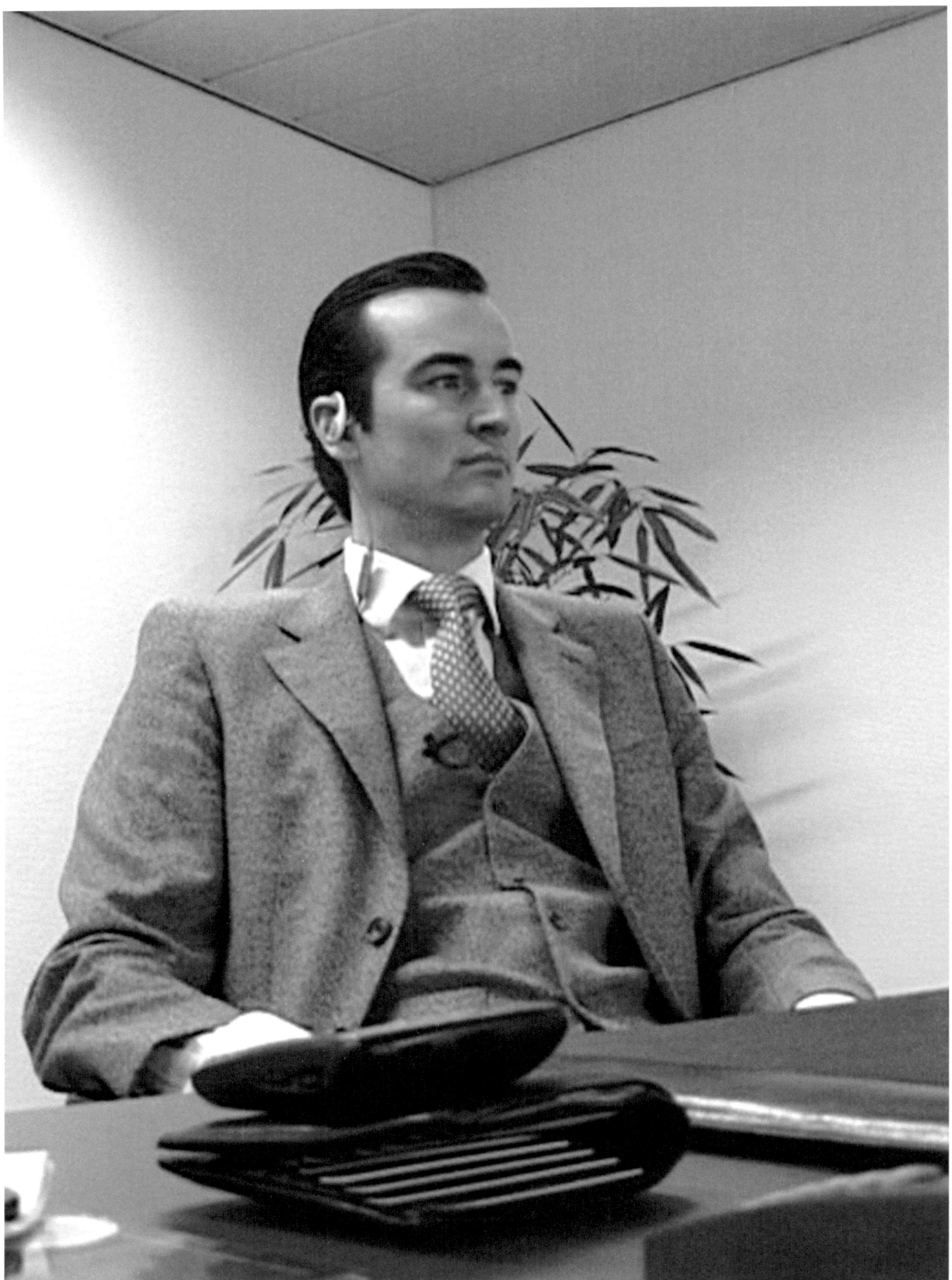

Read page 88

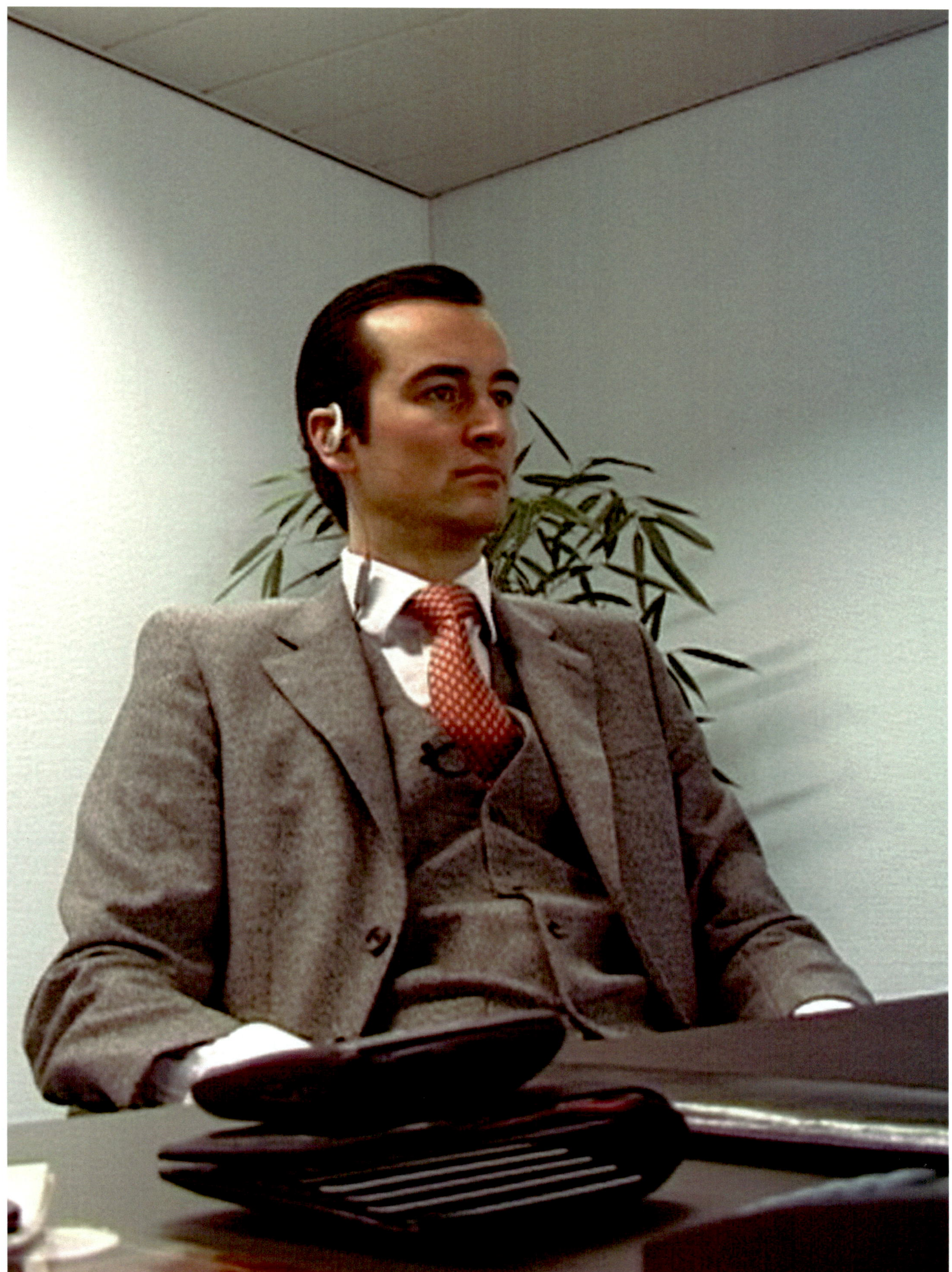

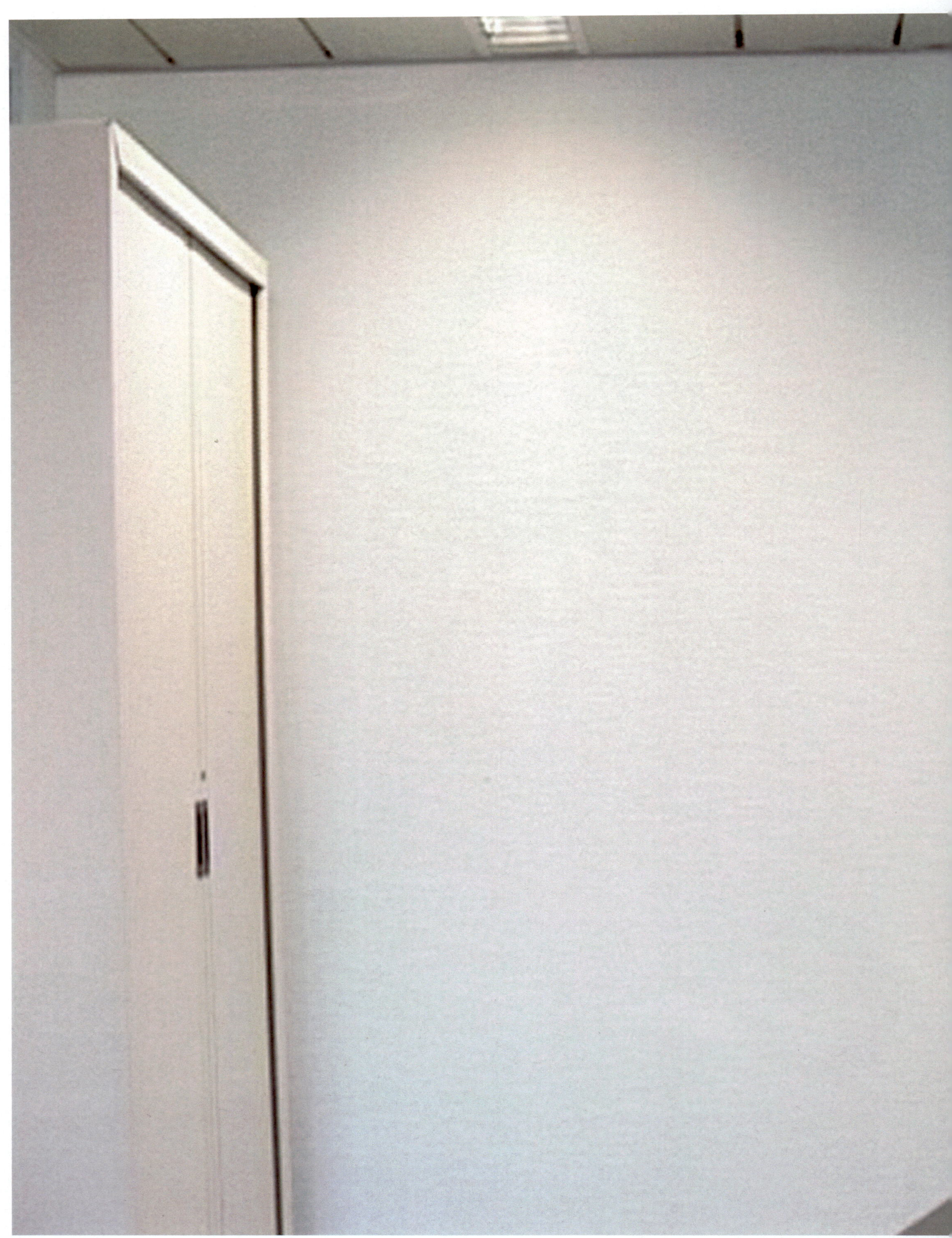

Read page 90

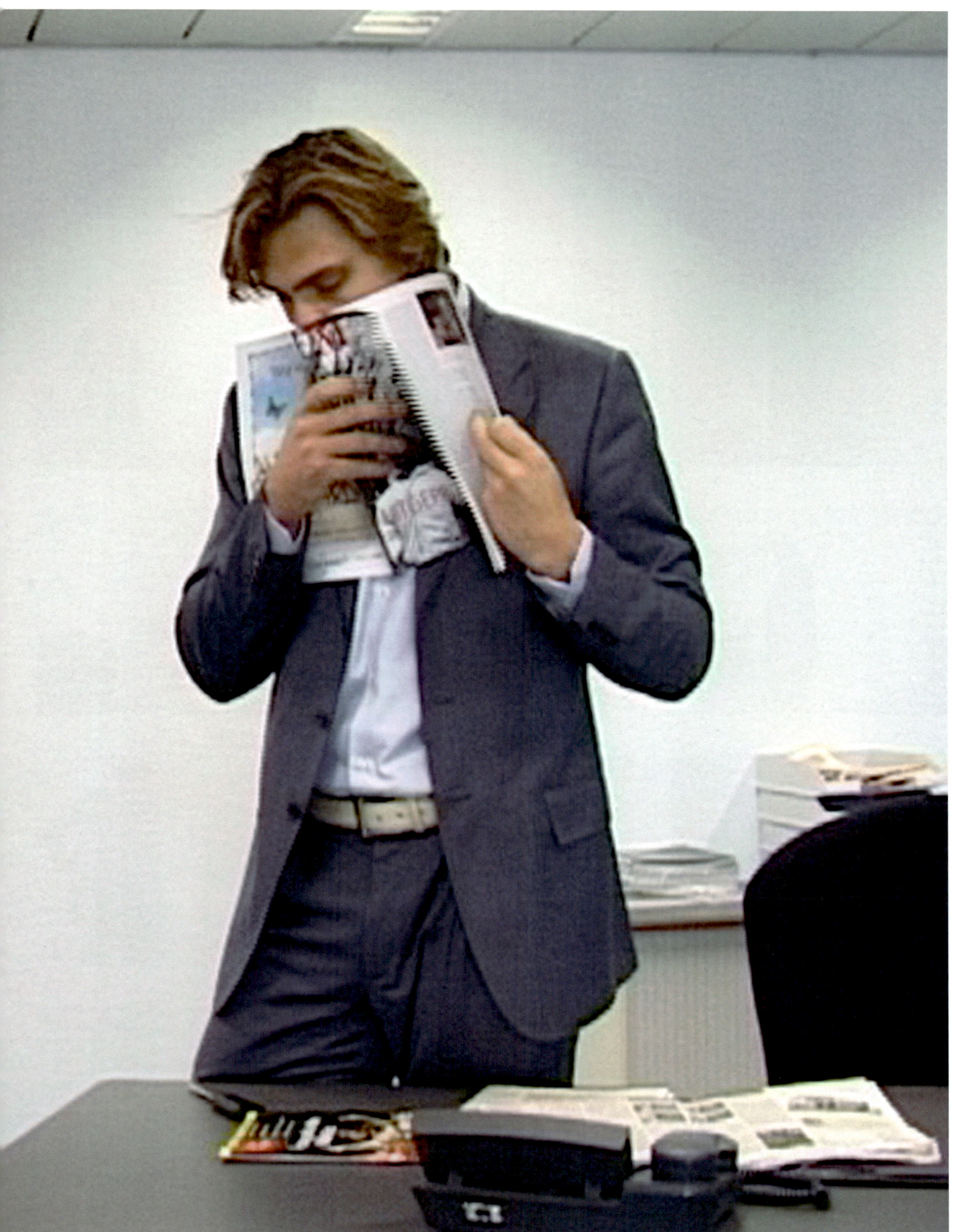

Recently, I was in a room where I was clearly the poorest. All the other guys had more than 100 million dollars.
Or euros. So I was the poorest. Someone always is.

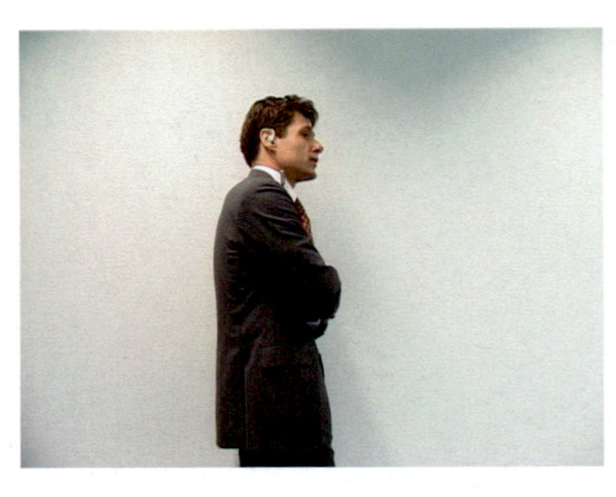
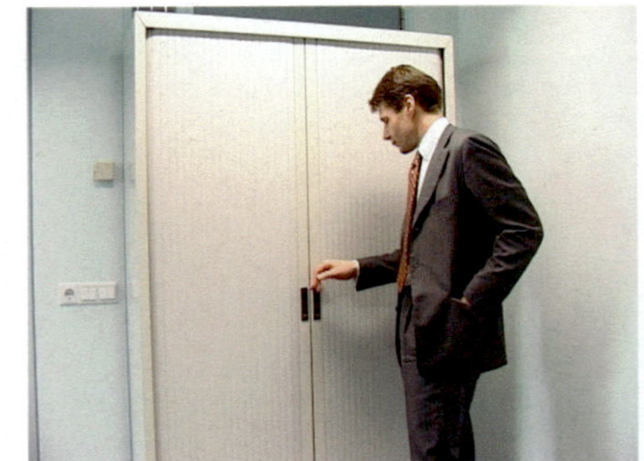
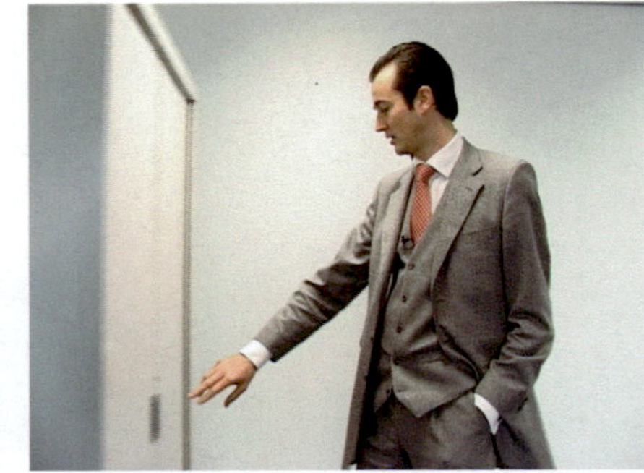
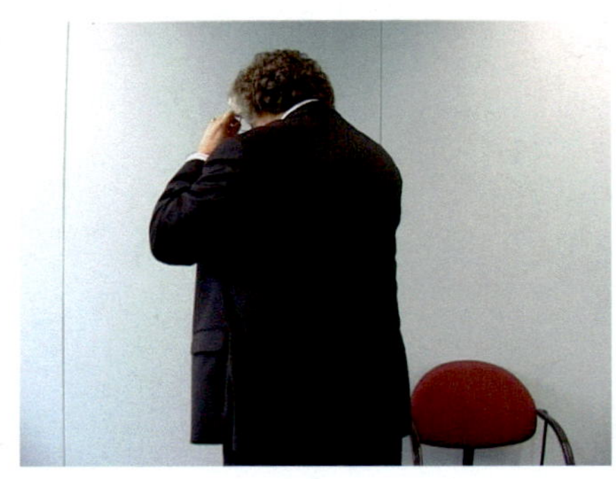
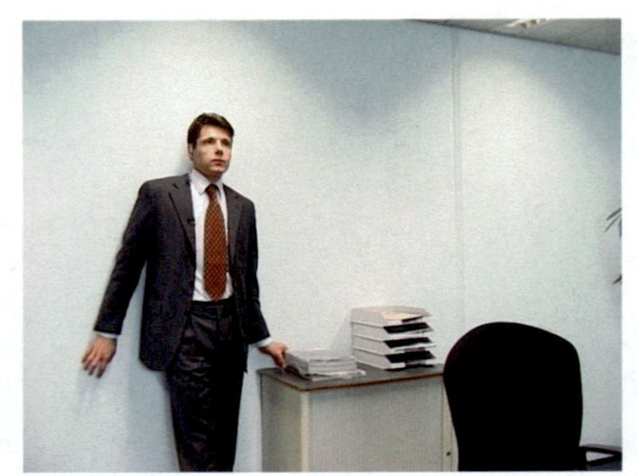
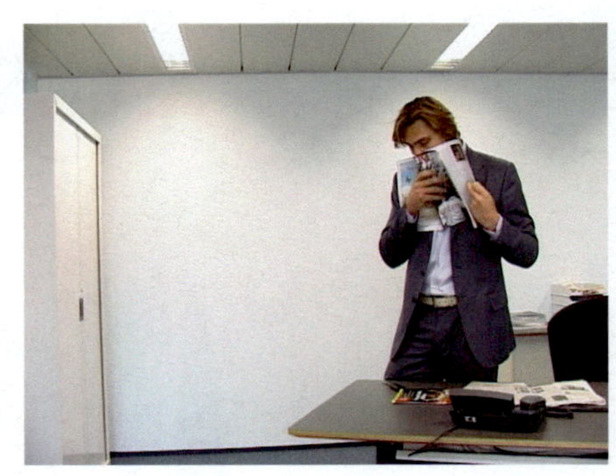
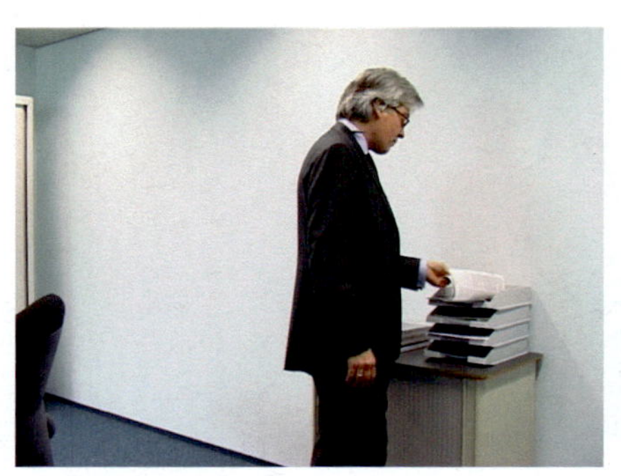
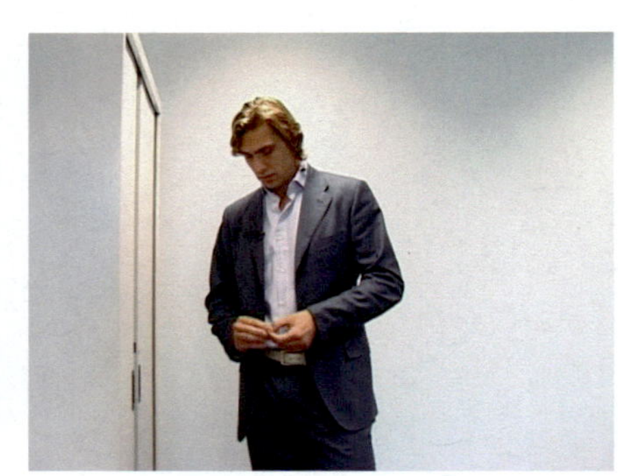
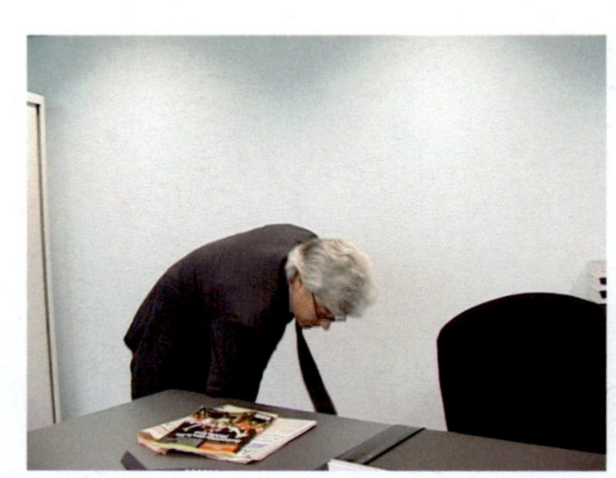
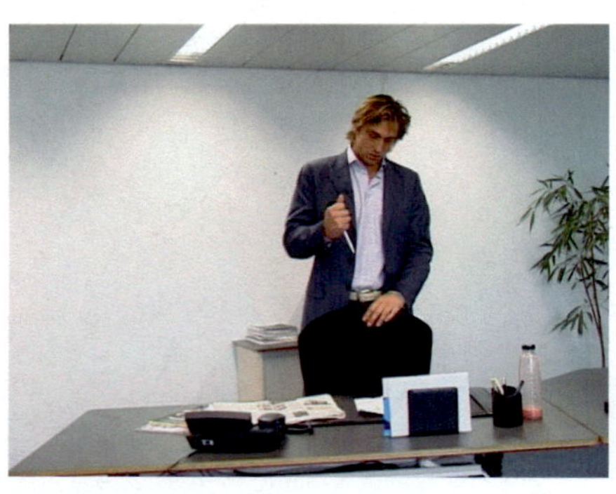
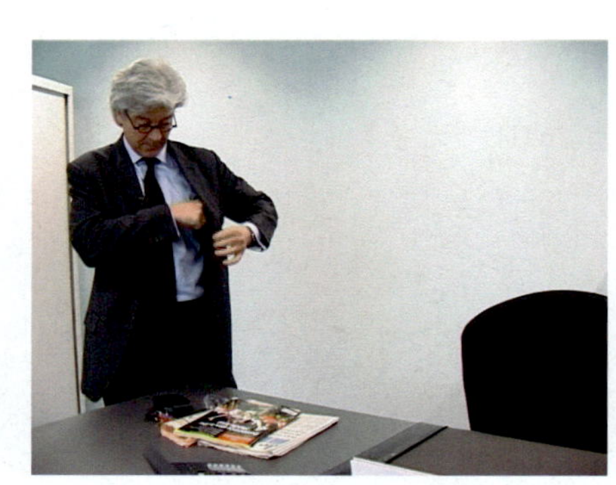
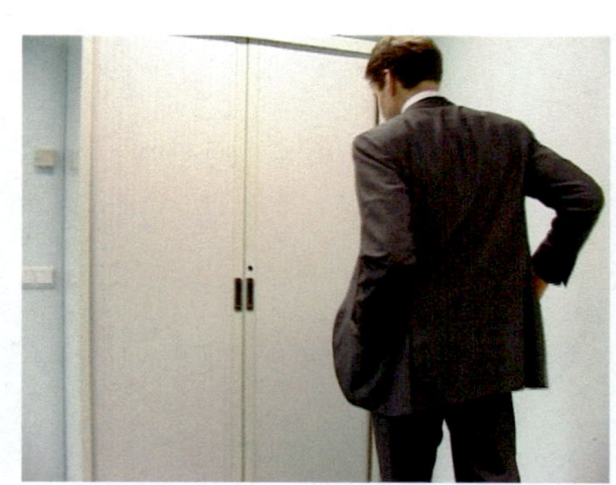
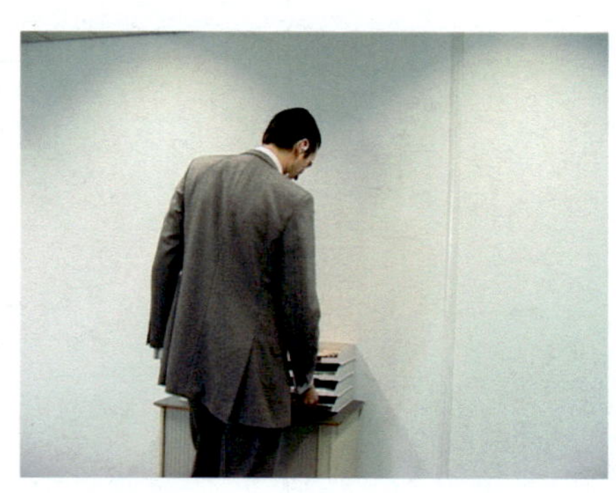
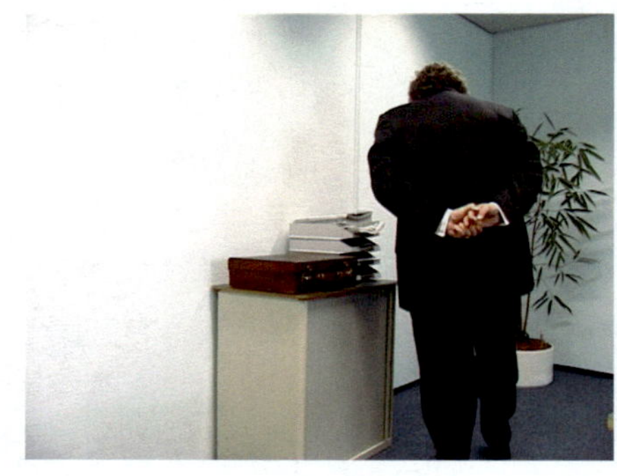
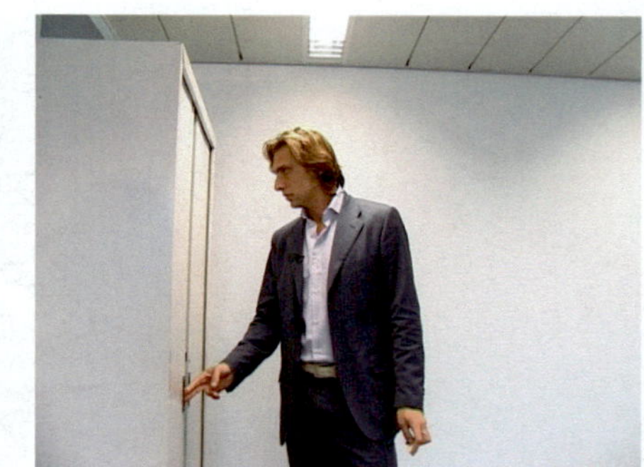

Read page 89

Video installation,
17:56 min, subtitled,
2 dvds, 2005

2 synchronized
projections, with
separate soundtracks
played via 4 speakers,
which are placed on the
opposite wall from the
projection

Camera: Bert Oosterveld
Concept: Julika Rudelius,
Martin Hansen
Editing: Martin Hansen
Subtitles: Erik Pezarro
Assistants: Jorgen
Karskens, Vincent van
de Waal, M.J. Kortmann
Research and advice:
David Mulder

Thanks to:
Daniela Petovic (KPN
Kunstzaken), Ton van der
Gaag (KPN Noordwest),
Marc-Jan van Laake,
Melle Daamen, Tilly
Hendrik-de Lange,
Margit Lucács,
Maartje Fliervoet,
Marty Lamers, Marieken
Verheyen and Helle
Lyshøj

ECONOMIC PRIMACY

VIDEO INSTALLATION
17:56 MIN
2 DVDs
SUBTITLED
2005

A generic corner office, blue carpet, desk with laptop and fruit bowl, a conference table with a Stelton thermos and coffee cups, four chairs, two plants, two cabinets of different sizes, no wall decoration, four windows looking out over other modern office buildings, a highway and a power plant in the distance. All the managers wear an earpiece.

LEFT SCREEN

RIGHT SCREEN

Boris, tall and slim, black hair combed back, wearing a three-piece light brown tweed suit, orange and red tie and a white button-down shirt, is seated at the desk

BORIS: I always wanted to be a million-aire. That takes a special kind of ambition. I often talk to businessmen, and I ask them why they do it. And they say that they like having a business or whatever. The reason doesn't matter, as long as it's an important one... Whether it's that your father hit you or that you're insecure with women, and you think that power and money will solve the problem. You have to be really motivated. Then the reason doesn't matter.

Boris from behind as he looks out the window and twiddles his fingers behind his back

Boris walks quickly to the cabinet, tries to poke his finger in between the doors, turns around, puts his hands into his pockets and walks towards the window

BORIS: Personally, I'd like to have lots of money. I think that money is very important. It's an important measurement standard. You can really use it to measure the value of something. Money is an independent measuring tool. Boris stands in front of the window and looks out. You can use it to measure anything. Not that it can measure everything. Love can't be expressed in money... But you can try.* 'How much do you love your boyfriend? If I gave you 10 million bucks, would you dump him?' Then it becomes a way to measure.

Ivo stands in front of the window and looks out

Boris stands in front of the cabinet

*See pages 82/83

LEFT SCREEN   RIGHT SCREEN

Jochem stands next to the cabinet
crumpling a small piece of paper

BORIS: You can use money to achieve
things. After that, it's a question of
how fast you're satisfied. Some say love
isn't for sale. And that's true... On the
other hand, if you're really poor you
have less of a chance to find love than if
you're filthy rich. Especially if you're
willing... to overlook the motives of
those who are attracted to you. He smiles.

Boris walks around eating a croissant

BORIS: I struggle with that a lot... I
don't know what I should do about Africa.*
I've been there, it interests me immensely
but I feel it's a lost cause. Even if some
African countries are doing OK and we
don't need to do anything there. But...
He looks out the window. I really don't
know what to do... He takes a bite of the
croissant. ...about Africa.

Ton leans on the window frame at the far
end of the office and stares out the window

Boris looks out the window, his hands
crossed behind him, then he starts walking
through the office

BORIS: It's inevitable that some people
are poor. Someone is always the poorest...
People shouldn't have to starve to death.
But... Recently, I was in a room where I
was clearly the poorest. All the other
guys had more than 100 million dollars.
Or euros. So I was the poorest. Someone
always is.** You can only hope that the
world as a whole will get richer and
that the poor will also get richer... In
Holland, almost no one starves to death.
Probably no one. So everything's fine.

Boris sits motionless at the desk, leaning
backwards and looking straight into the
room

Herman, medium height, short, light brown
hair, wearing a brown single-breasted
suit, red tie, white shirt, leans with his
back against the wall, his arms crossed

HERMAN: Well, I think... that according
to statistics I have an above-average
income. At the same time, I don't think...
I'm rich in the sense that money makes
me a powerful person... It does give me

Herman walks over to the small cabinet,
he looks at some files, then he turns,
trips and catches himself as he lands
against the wall

LEFT SCREENRIGHT SCREEN

more freedom than others have. But not to
the extent that... I've never been able
to reconcile myself with the fact that my
money gives me power over others.

Jochem leafs through a magazine. He puts
it under his nose and smells it*

Herman sits on the windowsill

HERMAN: So yes, to be honest, I do
have a certain amount of power and I
contribute to important decision-making.
But that's... He eats a grape, brings his
foot up to the windowsill and looks out
the window. My work has to have meaning.
I used to work in a big law firm that
dealt only with companies. After four
years, I'd had enough. It was too far
from my own idealistic ideas. I wanted
to become an all round lawyer. So I went
to work in a very small firm, with three
other people. I worked less, took care
of the kids one day a week. I went to
work for the simple folk who rang the
doorbell and who sat in the waiting room
with plastic bags full of problems. I had
enough of that quickly... To begin with,
I was earning less. But even worse, those

Herman pulls the chair toward him and sits
at the desk

HERMAN: I sometimes wonder if there are
people who... because I... He puts his
feet up on the drawers next to him.
I've never been flashy with my cash...
If you want to catch a wasp you have to
use honey. So if you want to attract a
beautiful woman... if that's your goal
you have to show your honey, your money,
to attract those wasps. But... I don't
need to do that, that's not my style but
I wonder if there are people who are
interested in that money.

Boris plucks some grapes from the fruit
bowl on the desk. One rolls off the table
and falls onto the floor. He bends down
to pick the grape up and eats it. Then he
wanders around the desk

*See pages 84/85

LEFT SCREEN   RIGHT SCREEN

people, as a colleague once told me: They come in, pull their pants down and shit all over your desk... Often, these people manage their affairs so badly... that you think, give me a break. Go figure it out for yourself. So within a year, I left. Mostly because I... One illusion fewer... I thought, great, pro bono work but because these people don't have the incentive to pay for their lawyer... I know laywers are very expensive, and it should be subsidized. But because they don't have to pay us themselves, you see that... Maybe society has to get tougher. I guess it's heading that way.*

Jochem, tall with a football player's build, shoulder-length blond hair nonchalantly combed back. He is wearing a medium-blue single-breasted suit with a light-blue shirt. The two top buttons are open. He sits at the desk

JOCHEM: I think... No, I'm sure that making money, and making even more money is reserved for very few people. Maybe for Warren Buffett. He's one of the most successful investors in the world. But most people don't know what to do with money... The only reason that money exists is to realize something else... Take a look at the world we live in. Look at the welfare system... A system in which when someone goes blank... and by blank, I mean he's sick, he can't function, he's not

Ivo sits at the desk, he brushes his suit off, the fingers of his left hand are tapping the desk, he leans back listening, rocking back and forth in the chair

Ton drinks coffee while walking towards the window, then he turns to put his cup back on the desk

Herman sits at the desk, listening, looking at a brochure. After a while, he looks up quickly, then he bends down and starts tinkering with the chest of drawers under the desk

*See page 2

<table>
<tr><td align="center">LEFT SCREEN</td><td align="center">RIGHT SCREEN</td></tr>
</table>

in the mood, etc... he gets money handed to him... So we've created a system that says, if you don't feel like working you just go to social services and get your monthly handout. And the better off you were, and the worse off you are now, the more you get. <u>He drinks fresh-squeezed fruit juice.</u> So it's a system that guarantees something that doesn't help anybody... It's like giving a diamond ring to a four-year-old. <u>He gets up.</u>

<u>Ivo stands at the small cabinet, leafing through a brochure and eating grapes</u>

<u>Jochem paces around the desk eating grapes</u>

JOCHEM: What sick or incapacitated person is really getting helped by getting a guaranteed sum of money* put on his account?... You have to figure that in this system, with almost 17 million people, one million declared unable to work, 600,000 jobless... <u>He picks up a letter opener and taps into his right hand to accentuate his speech.</u> We are talking about a sick system.

<u>Jochem stands behind the chair, his hands resting on the back of it</u>

JOCHEM: I know some beggars on the street. I always give them some money. 2 euros for a place to sleep? Why not? I go in my wallet and think, who am I to refuse this guy 2 euros? <u>He starts walking around the desk, brushing off the surface.</u> And for your handicapped girlfriend? I'll give her some money, too... No, it doesn't solve the problem. It's all about redistribution. I think that people who have a lot could have a little less.

<u>Ton sits at the desk with his hands crossed, looking straight ahead, listening</u>

<u>Jochem puts the point of the letter opener into the surface of the desk and walks around it</u>

JOCHEM: All of those people get quite a bit of money, the average is 1500 or 2000 euros per month, guaranteed... <u>He plays</u>

LEFT SCREEN   RIGHT SCREEN

Jochem walks towards the window listening, pulling at his lower lip

Jochem stops at the desk to drink some juice

JOCHEM: What I earn per month? Between 8000 and 9000 euros... Before taxes. Listens. Buy stuff... Invest... Earn even more.

Jochem walks around the office, tapping the letter opener at an accelerated pace into his hand

Ivo paces back and forth in front of the window, listening, plucking grapes off the stem

with the letter opener. If I take someone like my sister, who was declared unfit to work for seven years... If a couple years back, I had put her in the jungle, saying, here's your house, here are your two kids. Go find a way to feed them. He starts pacing. In no time, she'd have gone into action. She'd have found the strength to do it. She'd have found solutions, been creative and maybe even felt happy.

Boris leafs through a brochure on the small cabinet. He puts his hands behind his back and walks towards the back wall

Jochem paces around the office

JOCHEM: That's how this system works. People with more exclusive talents get more money. They're in demand. I have tons of work. The lowly secretary doesn't. Typists are a dime a dozen. Far fewer people have my kind of skills.

Ivo, medium height, suntanned, white 'boyish' hair, hornrimmed glasses. He is wearing a dark brown suit a light blue shirt and a bordeau red tie. He sits on the windowsill facing the office

IVO: Oh, everything! He starts pacing back and forth in front of the window. What can we satisfy with money in our society? I'm pragmatic. I'd say everything. Everything is for sale. In that sense,

LEFT SCREEN

RIGHT SCREEN

money has become the most valued good in our society. We depend on it, and we can achieve everything with it. Even power and image. It's ridiculous, but it's true. He sits on the windowsill again. So I think you can satisfy everything with money... They say money doesn't buy happiness. That's only partially true. Money does buy happiness because you can achieve anything with it, even an image boost. Or the power that comes along with it. Let's be honest.

IVO: I don't have the aura of a millionaire. Rather that of someone who is simply successful and who has money. He walks to the window, touches the curtains, adjusts his glasses, then he touches the windowsill.

Ivo leans with his back against the window

IVO: Yeah, that's not my department... I understand the motivation of anti-globalists. I also see that they have ideals, and that they have the right to such ideals. He sways back and forth. I don't accept their eternal negativity and criticism, without making a contribution. Their parasitic hold on society. Let's be honest...

Ivo leans against the window frame, looking out, his right hand in his pocket

IVO: ...these people can live their lives, can say and do what they like because there are rich people who keep the world economy going who ensure that trains run, planes fly and houses get built so that they can protest. They forget that... Their eternal negativity and their irresponsible resistance to anything that smells of money, is really thoughtless.

Jochem stands behind the desk, reading a newspaper, then he walks away

Ton, heavy build, graying curls, frameless glasses, is wearing a dark brown suit, white shirt and a brown, red, and yellow diagonally-striped tie. He sits at the desk, puts his coffee cup down, folds his hands and licks his lips.

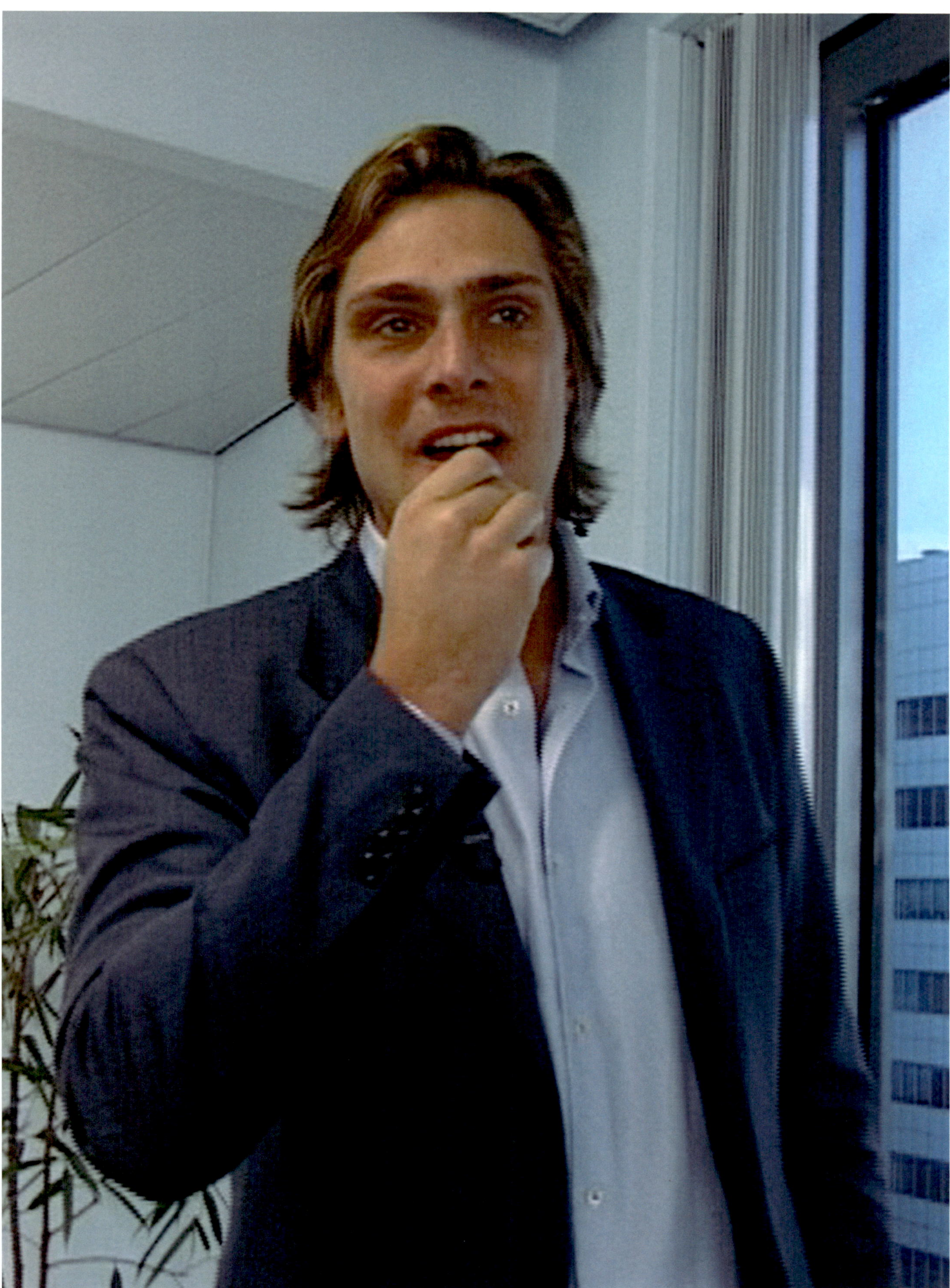

Read page 92

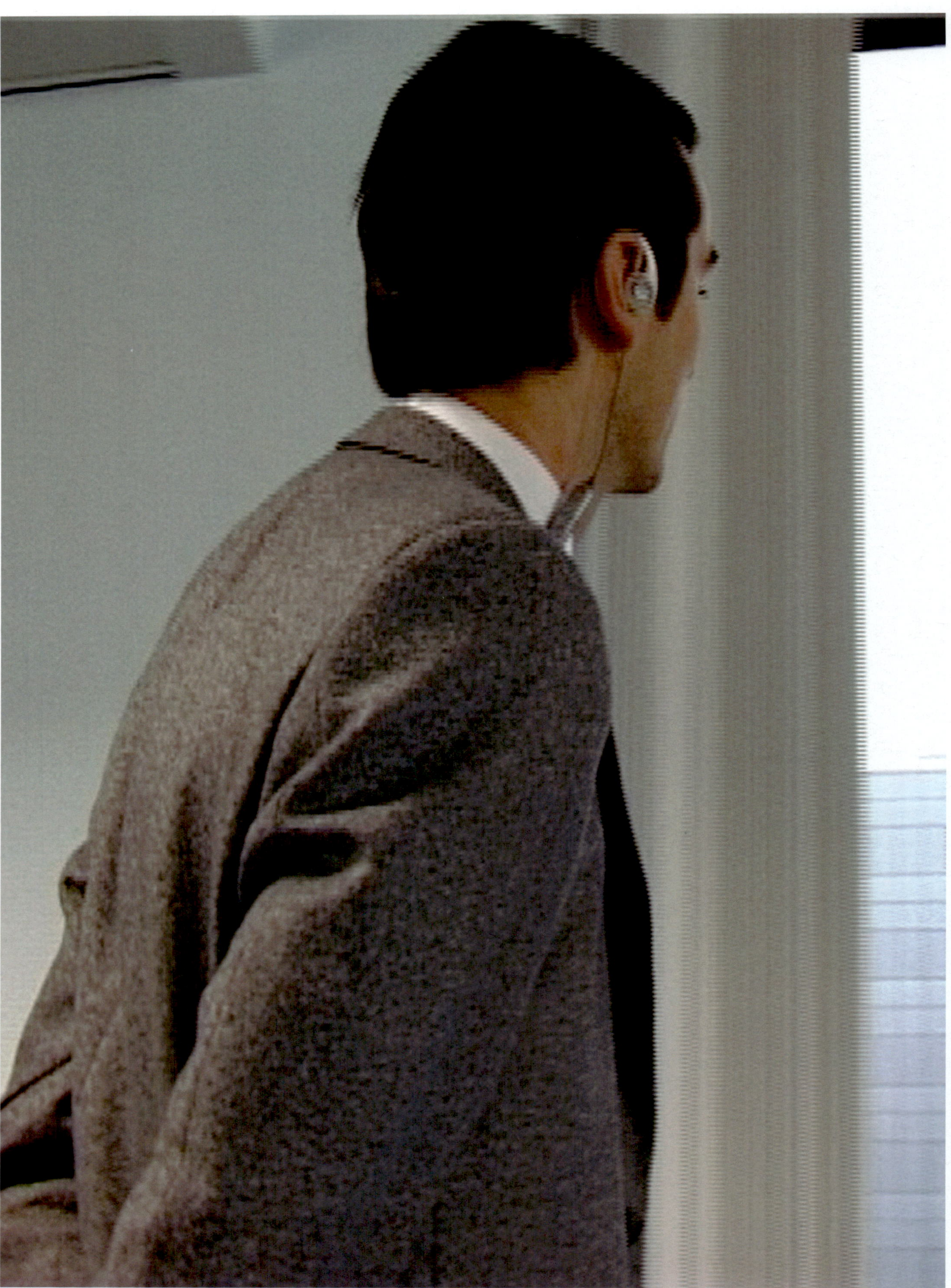

Read page 89

LEFT SCREEN   RIGHT SCREEN

TON: I can't bear to think of a world
without choices, with people who are all
the same... Everyone with the same amount
of money? Unimaginable! And above all,
let's face it: there are jobs in society
that simply have to get done and if
everyone earned the same, that wouldn't
happen... It's not a very popular thing to
say, but that's how it is. He picks up
his coffee cup and drinks from it.

Ton gets up and walks towards the window

TON: I truly believe that everyone can
earn money. There are lots of people in
real estate who haven't had a higher
education, and who still have made it big.
He paces in front of the windows. And
that happened because they were clever
and streetwise. They've come a long way.
They're independent and they do what they
like... So the idea that money isn't fair
He leans with both hands on the desk.
I don't buy it... Money is evenly
distributed throughout society.

Jochem walks towards the cabinet, plays
with the handle indentations, tries to
open it and walks back to the window

Ton stands with his back to the camera
facing the back wall, head down, hands
folded behind his back

TON: Pity... Independence... Education...
Agitated, he starts pacing around the
desk, gesticulating. We need to lose the
idea that people are pitiful.

Ton paces around the desk

TON: People can determine their own fate.
They can do something about it. That's
important. Money is only a means to an
end... Money is independence. It's only
something to help you get your affairs
in order. So that you're not dependent
on others. He stops briefly to put his
hands on the back of the chair, then
starts pacing again. The materialistic

Boris meanders around the plant, hands in
his pant pockets

LEFT SCREEN

RIGHT SCREEN

aspect is less important. Sure I like a
glass of good wine. I also like a good
restaurant, but that's not as important.
What's important is that you have your
independence... Enough of this culture of
pity. We have all these people on welfare
who take and take and take. They don't
deserve it. We have to inspect them and
get rid of them. He pauses at the window.
What should we do with that money? Pay our
nurses better. Pay our teachers better.
Take a look at education in Holland. It's
insanity! Teachers get next to nothing.
Education is an investment! We say it
but don't do anything about it. Children
and education, they're what's really
important.

Herman walks towards the cabinet, plays
with the handle indentations, listens

Ton paces, less agitated than before

Ton sits at the desk, listening. He takes
off his glasses, straightens his hair,
starts leafing through a magazine

TON: I took my kids to Egypt... To
Egypt... I took them to Egypt, and there
we walked around in the souks. I taught
them bargaining. It was fun. My daughter
was really tough. He laughs. It was
great. Really interesting... She's 13...
Just stuff she wanted to buy. I told
her to calculate their price in euros,
offer them a third and only go 10 percent
higher than that. No more. Then they will
respect you. Especially as a girl. And
she was sharp. She did it terrifically.

Ton paces in front of the window

TON: And that's true. Calculate a
third, then don't go higher than 10
percent. That's the way. Ton leans with
both hands on the back of the chair,
listening. That's up to you. I think
it's completely stupid to do that. He

Ivo quickly gathers his agenda, wallet,
keys and cell phone, puts them in his

LEFT SCREEN   RIGHT SCREEN

walks a couple of steps and leans over   pockets, bends down to get a plastic bag
the desk. If you walk away, they don't   and leaves
respect you. Another dumb western tourist.
But if you really bargain, and in the
end you say, 'Look me in the eyes!'
'Aren't you still earning something?'   Ton leans on the desk
Then they are honest and say yes.
                                                TON: Yeah, but that's life. Good
                                                intentions often go wrong. He walks
                                                towards the window and looks out. So!
                                                She's an idealist.

BIOGRAPHY
BIBLIOGRAPHY
COLOPHON

Julika Rudelius
Cologne (Germany), 1968
Lives in Amsterdam

<u>SOLO EXHIBITIONS</u>

2005

'Julika Rudelius. Vijf
videowerken 2001-2005',
Frans Hals Museum/De
Hallen, Haarlem, NL
(cat)

Studio Manuela Klerkx,
Milan, I

'Ansichten der Ökonomie/
Economic Primacy',
Kunstraum Lakeside,
curated by Hedwig
Saxenhuber, <u>Die Springer-
in</u>, Klagenfurt, Ö

2004

Galerie Reinhard Hauff,
Stuttgart, D

'Plus ou moins jeunes',
Centre Culturel Suisse,
Paris, F

'Feuilleton, deel
vijf', Marres, centrum
voor actuele kunst,
Maastricht, NL (cat)

'BijlmAir: Your Blood
is as Red as Mine',
Stedelijk Museum Bureau
Amsterdam/Artotheek
Zuidoost, Amsterdam, NL

2003

'You can't stay in the
80s wearing cowboy boots
while the whole world
progresses', Kunsthaus
Glarus, CH (cat)

Galerie Diana Stigter,
Amsterdam, NL

2001

'Talkshow', Stedelijk
Museum Bureau Amsterdam,
NL (cat)

<u>SELECTED GROUP
EXHIBITIONS</u>

2007 (planned)

Brooklyn Museum, New
York, USA

2006 (planned)

Kunsthalle Schirn,
Frankfurt a. M., D

2005

'Respect. Formes de
cohabitation', Musée
Dar Si Saïd, Marrakech,
M (cat)

'"A Second Sight".
International Biennale
of Contemporary Art
2005', National Gallery,
Prague, CZ (cat)

'Recreating the Case',
Kunsthaus Glarus, CH

'Migration', Kölnischer
Kunstverein, Cologne, D
(cat)

'Populism', Stedelijk
Museum Amsterdam, NL
(cat)

'Populism', Frankfurter
Kunstverein, Frankfurt
a. M., D (cat)

'Populism',The
Contemporary Art Center,
Vilnius, LIT (cat)

'Documentary
Strategies', TENT.
Centre for Visual Arts,
Rotterdam, NL (cat)

'Moving..on...
Handlungen an
Grenzen - Strategien
antirassistischen
Handeln', Neue
Gesellschaft für
Bildende Kunst, Berlin,
D (cat)

2004

'Untitled', Tate
Modern, London, UK

'Rheinschau - Art
Cologne Projects',
Rheinforum, Cologne, D,
organized by Stedelijk
Museum Bureau Amsterdam
'Histoire(s) Parallè-
le(s) création-confron-
tation France Pays-Bas',
Institut Néerlandais,
Paris, F (cat)

'Over zee, land en
gezicht', Museum Het
Valkhof, Nijmegen, NL

'Grenzeloos Kijken',
Film by the Sea Festival,
Scheveningen, NL

'Revisie', Dutch Film
Festival, Centraal
Museum, Utrecht, NL

'Antonietta Peeters,
Julika Rudelius en
Lily van der Stokker',
Stedelijk Museum,
Schiedam, NL

'Verworpenen en
zondagskinderen:
Aanwinsten 2003',
Frans Hals Museum,
Haarlem, NL

'Teenage Kicks.
Adolescence as subject',
The Gallery, Royal
Hibernian Academy,
Dublin, IR (cat)

'Wirklich wahr!
Realitätsversprechen
von Fotografien',
Ruhrlandmuseum, Essen,
D (cat)

'Art Rotterdam',
Galerie Diana Stigter,
Rotterdam, NL

'LISTE Basel', Kunsthaus
Glarus, Basel, CH

'Das zweite Bild',
dreizehnzwei, Wien, A /
Galerie Olaf Stüber,
Berlin, D (cat)

2003

'Link', Stedelijk
Museum Amsterdam, NL
(cat)

'Contemporary Dutch
Art', National Museum
of Contemporary Art,
Seoul, KR (cat)

'Strangers, The First
ICP Triennial of
Photography and Video',
International Center of
Photography, New York,
USA (cat)

'Utopie van de
periferie', Stedelijk
Museum Aalst, B

'Turbulence', Centre
for Contemporary Art,
Kiev, UKR (cat)

'Child in Time. Views of
contemporary artists on
youth and adolescence',
Gemeentemuseum Helmond,
NL (cat)

'Turbulence', Museum
voor Moderne Kunst,
Arnhem, NL

'Beyond beauty',
Galerie Diana Stigter,
Amsterdam, NL

2002

'Rendez-vous', Musée
d'Art Contemporain de
Lyon, F

'Faces, people and
society', Frans Hals
Museum, Haarlem, NL

'There's no accounting
for other peoples
relationships', Ormeau
Baths Gallery, Belfast,
IR

'Sold', Christie's,
Amsterdam, NL (cat)

'Non-Members only',
Arti et Amicitiae,
Amsterdam, NL

'Jong', De Beeldbank,
TU Eindhoven, NL

'LISTE Basel', Galerie
Diana Stigter, Basel, CH

'Dark Spring', Ursula
Blickle Stiftung,
Kraichtal, D (cat)

'Non Places',
Frankfurter Kunstverein,
Frankfurt a. M., D (cat)

'A'dam & Eve', De
Appel, Amsterdam, NL

'The People's Art',
Witte de With, Rotterdam
(cat)

2001

'You never walk alone',
Stroom, Haags centrum
voor beeldende kunst,
The Hague, NL

'Commitment, een keuze
uit drie jaar Fonds
BKVB', Las Palmas,
Rotterdam, NL (cat)

'From Here to Reality
- a dutch show', Index
The Swedish Contemporary
Art Foundation,
Stockholm, S (cat)

'A Arte do Povo',
Central Eléctrica do
Freixo, Porto, P

2000

'For Real', Stedelijk
Museum, Amsterdam, NL
(cat)

'Hellenistic', W139,
Amsterdam, NL

'Scripted Spaces', Witte
de With, Rotterdam, NL

'Man muss ganz schön
viel lernen um hier
zu funktionieren',
Frankfurter Kunstverein,
Frankfurt a. M., D

EXHIBITION CATALOGUES
(A SELECTION)

2005

Respect! Formes de
cohabitation/Vormen van
samenleven, Amsterdam:
Mondriaan Foundation

International Biennale
of Contemporary Art,
Prague: National
Gallery, pp. 572-573

Projekt Migration,
Cologne: Kölner Kunst-
verein, pp. 196-197

The Populism Catalogue,
Berlin/New York: Lukas
& Sternberg

Frits Gierstberg et
al. (eds), Documentary
now!, Rotterdam: NAi
Publishers, p. 30

Moving on. Border
Activism - Strategies
for Anti-Racist Actions,
Berlin: Bildwechsel/
Neue Gesellschaft für
Bildende Kunst

2004

Erik Kessels, Gabriel
Bauret, Histoire(s)
Parallèle(s) création
- confrontation France
Pays-Bas, Paris:

Filigranes Éditions

Teenage Kicks,
adolescence as subject,
Dublin: Royal Hibernian
Academy

Sigrid Schneider,
Stefanie Grebe (eds),
Wirklich wahr!
Realitätsversprechen von
Fotografien, Ostfildern
(Ruit): Hatje Cantz

Das zweite Bild, text
by Melanie Ohnemus,
Wien: dreizehnzwei

2003

You can't stay in the
80s wearing cowboy
boots while the whole
world progresses,
interview by Jan van
Adrichem, Glarus: Kunst-
haus Glarus

We Show Art, 10 Years
Stedelijk Museum Bureau
Amsterdam, Amsterdam:
Artimo, pp. 497-508

Link, Amsterdam:
Stedelijk Museum
Amsterdam/Rotterdam:
NAi Publishers

XL Photography 2, Art
Collection Deutsche
Börse, Ostfildern
(Ruit): Hatje Cantz

In or Out, Contemporary
Dutch Art, Amsterdam:
Canvas Foundation/
Seoul: Yellow Sea

Cultural Network
Edward Earle et al.
(eds), Strangers, The
First ICP Triennial of
Photography and Video,
New York: International
Center of Photography/
Göttingen: Steidel

Turbulence, Arnhem:
Museum voor Moderne
Kunst

Prix de Rome 2003,
Art and Public Space,
Rotterdam: 010 Pub-
lishers

Frank Hoenjet, Linda
Modderkolk, Child in
Time. Visies van heden-
daagse kunstenaars op

jeugd en adolescentie,
Helmond: Gemeentemuseum
Helmond

2002

There's No Accounting
for Other People's
Relationships, text by
Suzanna Chan, Belfast:
Ormeau Baths Gallery
(leaflet)

Siebren de Haan,
'Cosmo Pubers', in:
Regionalisten, Nijmegen:
Paraplufabriek/
Amsterdam: VRIZA

Lex ter Braak, Edwin
Jansen, Commitment, een
keuze uit drie jaar
Fonds BKVB, Amsterdam:
Fonds voor beeldende
kunsten, vormgeving en
bouwkunst

Nabeelden. Album van
niet gemaakte foto's,
Amsterdam: De Balie

Dark Spring, Kraichtal:
Ursula Blickle Stiftung

Non places, New York:
Lukas & Sternberg

2001

From Here to Reality,
Stockholm: Index The
Swedish Contemporary
Art Foundation

The People's Art/A Arte
do Povo, Rotterdam:
Witte de With/Porto:
Central Eléctrica do
Freixo

This is for real,
Amsterdam: Stedelijk
Museum Amsterdam/
NAi Publishers,
Rotterdam

Charles Esche,
'Talkshow', Nieuwsbrief
Stedelijk Museum Bureau
Amsterdam no. 64

ARTICLES (A SELECTION)

2004

Kees Keijer,
'Schildenpadden en
speldenprikjes', Het
Parool (PS van de week)
25 October 2004

Barbara van Erp, 'Ik
kijk door de ogen van
een witte trut', Vrij
Nederland 1 May 2004

Douglas Heingartner,
'Julika Rudelius',
Flash Art January, 2004

2003

Maria Barnas, 'En ik
dan', De Groene Amster-
dammer 2 August 2003

Martine van Kampen,
Jaap Vinken, 'Reality-
art', Tubelight nr. 29,
November 2003

Jacquine van Elsberg,
'Ik ga er niet bij lopen
als een crimineeltje',
Skrien November 2003
p. 55

2002

Vanessa Joan Müller,
'Focus auf Julika
Rudelius', Frankfurter
Rundschau Magazin 13
April 2002

2001

Sjoukje Posthuma, 'De
raadselachtige video's
van Julika Rudelius',
BLVD December 2001

Maartje Somers,
'Tussen echt en nep,
gedragsexperimenten van
Julika Rudelius', NRC
Handelsblad (CS) 14
December 2001

2000

Jacquine van Elsberg,
'Art house, Julika
Rudelius', Skrien no.
240, February 2000

TELEVISION BROADCASTING

2004

Julika Rudelius
documentary RAM, VPRO
television, 25 April
2004

Metrópolis, Televisión
Española, viewing of
The highest point and
Tagged

SCREENINGS AT VIDEO
FESTIVALS (A SELECTION)

European Media Art
Festival, Osnabrück, D

Ann Arbor Film Festival,
USA

Impakt Festival,
Utrecht, NL

9th Rio de Janeiro
International Short
Film Festival, BR

International Film
Festival, MEDIAWAVE, HR

Festival International
du Film d'Amiens, F

Bandits Images,
Bourges, F

Lux, Nijmegen, NL

2nd Annual Detroit
International Video
Festival, Museum of New
Art, Detroit, USA

Maison Européenne de la
Photographie, Paris, F

Nederlands Film
Festival, Utrecht, NL

International Festival
of New Film, Split, HR

Video festival,
National Cinema Museum,
Turin, I

DISTRIBUTION (VIDEO)

Montevideo, Time Based
Arts, Amsterdam, NL

COMMISSIONS

2001

Photo works for Oost
Kunst/East Art, Kunst
in het Oostelijk Haven-
gebied van Amsterdam
/ Art in Amsterdam's
Eastern Docks Area,
010 Publishers,
Rotterdam, NL

2000

Video and stills
produced for SKOR/
Annual Report 2000
Amsterdam, NL

1998

Illustration of the
Annual Report of the
Council for Culture
(Raad voor Cultuur),
NL: with the photo
work: Without title '98

GRANTS/PRIZES

2004

Nederlands Film
Festival, special
mention Dutch film
critics for Tagged

2000

KLM (Royal Dutch
Airlines), Amsterdam

1999

Robert Bosch Stiftung,
Stuttgart

RESIDENCIES

2006

Residency at ISCP, NYC,
USA

2003

BijlmAir residency from
Stedelijk Museum Bureau
Amsterdam/Artotheek
Zuidoost, NL

1999-2001

Residency at the
Rijksakademie van
beeldende kunsten,
Amsterdam, NL

COLLECTIONS
(A SELECTION)

Art Collection
Deutsche Börse,
Frankfurt a. M., D

Bergsma, Amsterdam, NL

Frans Hals Museum,
Haarlem, NL

KPN Telecom, The Hague,
NL

Museum voor Moderne
Kunst, Arnhem, NL

Rabobank Nederland,
Eindhoven, NL

Stedelijk Museum
Amsterdam, NL

The publication Julika
Rudelius, Looking at
the Other coincides
with the exhibition
'Julika Rudelius. Vijf
videowerken 2001-2005'
at De Hallen, Haarlem
(NL), 17 December 2005-
26 February 2006.

This publication was
made possible by the
generous support of:
the Mondriaan Founda-
tion, Amsterdam

De Hallen, Haarlem
www.dehallen.com

Galerie Diana Stigter,
Amsterdam
www.dianastigter.nl

Nederlands Instituut
voor Mediakunst,
Montevideo/Time Based
Arts, Amsterdam
www.montevideo.nl

Veenman drukkers,
Rotterdam
www.veenmandrukkers.nl

Julika Rudelius is
represented by Galerie
Diana Stigter, Amsterdam

AUTHORS
Sven Lütticken,
Julika Rudelius

COMPILATION
Julika Rudelius,
Thomas Buxó

GRAPHIC DESIGN
Thomas Buxó
www.buxo.nl

FONT
Library Mono
Laurenz Brunner
www.lineto.com

COPY EDITING
Els Brinkman,
Andrew Maggiore,
Laura Watkinson

LITHOGRAPHY AND PRINTING
Veenman drukkers,
Rotterdam

PUBLISHER
Valiz Publishers,
Amsterdam www.valiz.nl

CREDITS OF THE IMAGES
All video stills and
installation views

by Julika Rudelius,
except:
page 11 top: Tobias
Zielony
page 11 bottom: Marc
Domage

Available in the
Netherlands, Belgium
and Luxemburg through
Centraal Boekhuis,
Culemborg; Scholtens,
Sittard and Coen
Sligting Bookimport,
Amsterdam, NL,
sligting@xs4all.nl,
fax +31-(0)20-6640047

Available in Europe
(except Benelux, UK
and Ireland), Asia and
Australia through Idea
Books, Amsterdam, NL,
idea@ideabooks.nl,
fax +31-20-6209299,
www.ideabooks.nl

Available in the
United Kingdom and
Ireland through Art
Data, London, UK,
orders@artdata.co.uk,
fax +44-208-742 2319,
www.artdata.co.uk

Available in the
USA: DAP, New York,
dap@dapinc.com,
fax (+1) 212-6279484,
www.artbook.com

www.valiz.nl
www.rudelius.org

NUR: 642, 640
ISBN 90-78088-05-2

Printed and bound in
the Netherlands

Mondriaan Stichting
(Mondriaan Foundation)